LANGUAGE AND LIBERATION
Creole Language Politics
In The Caribbean

by Hubert Devonish

Karia Press

Language and Liberation
Creole Language Politics in the Caribbean

First published in 1986 by **Karia Press.**
Copyright © Hubert Devonish, 1986.

Front cover illustration by Glenroy Sulle Caesar.
Cover design by Buzz Johnson.
Book design and layout by Buzz Johnson.
Typeset by **Karia.**

ISBN 0 946918 27 9 Pb.
ISBN 0 946918 27 8 Hb.

Karia Press,
BCM Karia,
London, WC1N 3XX.
United Kingdom.

Made and printed in Great Britain by the
Guernsey Press Co. Ltd., Guernsey, Channel Islands.

Acknowledgements

I would wish to acknowledge the contributions of the numerous People who, in one way or another, helped in the development of the ideas contained in this work. I would wish to single out a few for special mention: Shahin Owrang with whom the idea for a book like this was first discussed, Carol Davis who helped create the situation in which the idea for the book was born and who, several years later, encouraged its eventual completion and submission for publication, and Jean-Charles Pochard and Hilary Beckles with whom many of the issues dealt with in this volume were discussed at great length.

I would wish, also, to thank the University of the West Indies, and the Department of Linguistics and Use of English at the Mona Campus, for allowing me the study leave to take up a Commonwealth Academic Staff Fellowship at the School of Oriental and African Studies, London. Part of the period of the fellowship was spent putting finishing touches to the work and arranging publication. In this regard, I would also wish to thank the Commonwealth Scholarship Commission for having granted me the fellowship.

Hubert Devonish
January, 1986

Contents

Introduction

As someone living in the Caribbean in the late 20th century, as a person involved in the field of Linguistics, and as a native-speaker of Guyanese Creole, I find myself particularly interested in two related contemporary issues. The first of these is the means by which it will become possible to free the countries of the Caribbean from external political and economic control. It is clear that an essential part of this process will involve the creation of a new and genuine democracy. Such a democracy would allow the ordinary people of the Caribbean, the poor and the dispossessed, to control the societies in which they live. It is this freeing of the people of the region which is intended by the use of the term 'national liberation'. The second issue, closely related to the first, concerns the role which Creole languages, the ordinary everyday language of millions of people across the region, can and should play in the process of national liberation.

This work tries to tackle the second of the two issues. In order to deal with concrete, local and immediate questions, this work uses the technique of moving from the very general to the very specific in a series of stages. In Chapter 1, we look at the interaction between the way that human societies have developed through history, and the way that language status and functions have been involved in these developments. The focus narrows slightly in Chapter 2, which examines the language question as it has been raised in the course of socialist revolutions, as well as in certain post-colonial Third World countries. By Chapter 3 our concerns become even more specific as we begin to deal with the Caribbean by way of an examination of the Creole language question as it has developed through the centuries. It is only with a proper historical perspective that we can usefully analyse contemporary language issues in the region.

Chapter 4 deals with the contemporary Creole-speaking Caribbean, and particularly those situations in which the social and political struggle over the status and functions of Creole languages is most obvious.

The following chapter zeroes in on the case of the English-lexicon Creole languages of the Commonwealth Caribbean. In these situations, the struggle over language issues is a lot less obvious, much more subtle, but nevertheless very much present. It is particularly with reference to such societies that specific suggestions and recommendations are made in Chapter 6. These proposals are aimed at identifying what official language policies and practices would be appropriate in order to help achieve the goal of national liberation. The suggestions and recommendations put forward here, however, tend to lean in the direction of what should be done in circumstances where a movement aiming at achieving this goal is already in control of state power. Of course, state power in the Commonwealth Caribbean, is not, at present, in the hands of any such movement. Chapter 7, therefore, looks at the here and now, in the form of an examination of what should be done in the circumstances prevailing in a particular Caribbean country, Guyana. We try, in this chapter, to establish the importance of dealing with the language questionn even when those in favour of national liberation hold no state power. In the concluding chapter, we look at the Grenada experience. The failure of Grenada Revolution to deal with the Creole language question, and the difficulties which resulted from this failure, are not surprising. They are largely a reflection of the neglect of the Creole language question which has traditionally existed within left-wing and nationalist intellectual traditions in the Commonwealth Caribbean.

Caribbean linguists working in areas connected with language planning and language policy, have largely tended to operate with a supposedly value-free framework. They view their task as simply to describe and analyse language problems, and to recommend solutions within the strictures laid down by the existing social, political and economic order. This work is aimed at filling gaps in the approaches of (i) those who have a political and socio-economic perspective on the question of national liberation in the Caribbean but lack an insight into the language question, and (ii) those involved in fields of language planning and language policy who lack a perspective which integrates the language question into the overall debate about the political and socio-economic transformation of the Caribbean.

CHAPTER 1.

The Language Question and Human Society: A Historical Perspective

One area in which class conflict expresses itself in language is in the relationship between the language(s) used as the medium of informal spoken communication among the mass of the population, and the language(s) used for official purposes by the State and those who control it. In many cases, part of the explanation for the divergence in the language varieties used for these two sets of functions lies in the central role which writing plays in official language use. The ruling classes who control the State apparatus and language use within it, tend to identify themselves with the written form of the language, and attempt to model their own speech on this language form. This process is promoted by institutions such as the school system, which attach notions such as those of 'correctness' and 'beauty' to the written language. This effort to model ruling class speech behaviour on the written form of the language is usually only partially successful, since another factor is also at work. The written language form becomes transformed over time under the influence of the language spoken by the ruling classes. Nevertheless, it would be true to say that ruling class language, partly because it is influenced by the usually conservative and outdated written form of the language, tends to diverge from the more popularly used varieties, and therefore becomes distinct.

The concept of 'diglossia', developed by Ferguson (1959) and extended in its scope by Fishman (1971) and others, is extremely relevant here. The term 'diglossia' is used to describe a situation in which there exists two separate language varieties, each with its own specific functions within the society. The 'High' language variety in a diglossic situation is the language variety used in writing, in education, in government administrative and legal institutions, and generally in Public and Formal situations. These are largely domains which are dominated by and under the control of the ruling classes and their values. On the other hand, the 'Low' variety in a diglossic situation is the one used by the mass of the population in the course of their everyday private and informal interaction, within the family, and in the various forms of popular culture. Diglossia may involve either two dialects of the same language or two quite distinct languages altogether.

My view is that class conflict expresses itself in diglossic situations by way of the distribution of functions between the two language varieties involved. This distribution serves to exclude the mass of the population, who, of course, only speak the 'Low' variety, from the domains dominated by the ruling classes where only the 'High' variety is normally used. This chapter will examine, from a historical point of view, the way in which the related issues of diglossia and official language policy, have been dealt with in a variety of societies. Out of this, I hope, will come a theory about the relationship between diglossia and official language policy, on one hand, and the economic and social systems within which they exist, on the other. This may ultimately form the basis for the development of an approach to what should constitute a language policy which could most effectively help achieve the goals of socio-economic and political liberation, particularly in countries of the Third World, and more specifically, the Caribbean.

Diglossia and Official Language Policy in Pre-Capitalist Societies

Ancient Egypt and China provide the earliest examples of centralised and integrated nation states in human history. These societies were based on a large rural pesantry who paid taxes, in the form of their agricultural surplus, to a tiny state class who controlled the entire society. In order to administer nation states which they controlled, the state class in each of these societies set up a large, centralised state bureaucracy. This bureaucracy had the task of collection tax from the peasant producers, running a military apparatus for the protection of the peasantry from external attack, and organising large scale public works, notably those connected with irrigation. A section of the bureaucracy also carried out religious functions, religion being regarded as an arm of the state.

In any system of administration as complex as those existing in Ancient Egypt and China, the question of language use within the system was of great importance. This is illustrated by the fact that, in China, state planning of language goes back to 213 B.C. It was at this time that Li Si unified Chinese written characters as part of the unification of China taking place during that period under Chin Shi Huang Di. Li Si also established uniform terminology and standard forms of discourse for official correspondence and public documents. (Lehmann, 1975, p.42). In spite of the early date of this language planning exercise, the evidence suggests that diglossia had entrenched itself in China long before this period. Latourette (1946, p.774) states that there was a time during the Chou dynasty around 1000 B.C., when written Chinese at least approximated to the colloquial language of the period. The divergence between the written language and colloquial Chinese after this period can be explained by the fact that the spoken language continued to evolve as a result of the natural process of language change, whereas the written form of the language tended to remain relatively fixed and static. This diglossia between *weu-li* or Classical Chinese and colloquial varieties of the language continued right up to the beginning of the 20th century. It has displayed a remarkable stability throughout almost the entire period of the existence of China as a nation state.

The case of Ancient Egypt provides an interesting contrast. Here too diglossia made its appearance very early on in the process of the development of the state structure, as the language of informal spoken interaction changed while the written language remained static. However, instead of a single stable diglossia lasting for the entire period of Egyptian history, a new diglossia tended to emerge at each major stage in the nation's history. Thus, within the recorded history of Ancient Egypt, several quite distinct literary languages, Primitive Egyptian, Old Egyptian, Middle Egyptian and Coptic, followed each other into official written usage before dying out and being replaced by another. (Sotiropoulos, 1982, p. 3) This succession of officially used written languages occurred within the context of a specific kind of political history. From the establishment of the Egyptian state around 3000 B.C. onwards, several very distinct phases of Egyptian political history unfolded. There was the earliest period, prior to what is known as the Old Kingdom. There was then the Old Kingdom period itself, the Middle Kingdom period and the period of a New Kingdom (Butzer, 1978, pp. 37-41) Eact of these historical phases through which the Egyptian state passed tended to coincide with the pre-dominance of one of the official written languages mentioned above. As Sotiropoulos (1982, p.3) points out, these official written languages tended to be very conservative throughout the period in which they were used as official languages, whereas the spoken forms on which they were originally based kept on evolving naturally. This, therefore, resulted in the development of diglossia. This diglossia, however, only lasted until the time of a major political upheaval within the state leading to the replacement of the old ruling class by a new one. At this state, the diglossia associated with the previous political order was swept away, and a new official written language introduced which corresponded much more closely to the spoken language of the day. This new official written language would itself become static with the passage of time, diverging from the spoken language, and in its turn, a new diglossia would emerge.

But why was a single diglossia maintained in China throughout almost its entire history, while Ancient Egypt experienced a succession of diglossias? China, like Ancient Egypt, was success-fully over-run by several sets of invaders. This resulted in significant changes in the composition of its ruling class at various times in history. Thus, continuity in the composition of the Chinese ruling class throughout its history could hardly be put forward as an explanation for the continuity of its diglossia. Some historical facts do provide a clue, however. Accounts of Chinese history, notably those of Fitzgerald (1961) and Schirokauer (1978), suggest that foreign conquerors of China tended to inherit, relatively intact, the administrative bureaucracy of the preceding period. They usually just grafted their new administration on to the bureaucratic structure which they inherited. It was, of course, members of the administrative bureaucracy who were the major users of the official language in the course of their day-to-day activities. Thus, the relative continuity of the Chinese administrative bureaucracy, regardless of the identity of the ruling class, may explain the preservation of a fairly stable form of official language and the diglossia with which it was connected.

In the case of Egypt, however, according to the analysis of Butzer (1978, pp. 37-41), major changes in the make-up of the ruling class during its early history were usually preceded by long periods of economic and political decline, lasting hundreds of years. The periods of decline were caused by ecological disasters, involving either drought or massive yearly flooding from the Nile. According to Butzer, with an improvement in the ecological conditions, a new ruling class, often an invader, would appear on the scene to re-unite the nation state and re-establish a centralised state administration. In these circumstances,it is clear that the new rulers would not have been in a position to inherit much of an administrative bureaucracy from the preceding periods, nor to inherit much of the official language usage either. It seems, therefore, that what emerged in each period when a new ruling class rose to dominate Ancient Egypt, was a new official written language based on the contemporary speech of the new ruling class and propagated by members of the new administrative bureaucracy created to administer the state.

The difference between the official language history of China and Ancient Egypt seems to lie in the extent of the continuity of the administrative bureaucracy in these two nation states. The importance of bureaucratic classes in preserving and propagating diglossia is an issue which will re-appear again when we look at diglossia and official language policy in other types of society.

Diglossia and Official Language Policy in the Formation of Developed Capitalist Societies

We will examine in some detail the link between diglossia and official language policy, on one hand, and the emergence of capitalist domination of the state, using France as the major example. The reason is the radical and drastic nature of the French Revolution which brought the bourgeoisie of that country into control of the state. This caused an equally radical and drastic shift in official language policy and practice in the period after the revolution as compared with the period before it.

In the period up to the French Revolution in 1789, the vast majority of the population of France were native-speakers of language varieties other than French, and had little or no knowledge of that language. The Ordinance of 1539, instituting the use of French in place of Latin as the official language in the administration of justice, the administration of the State, etc. had two effects. Firstly, by making French the official language in place of Latin, those sectors of the ruling class whose knowledge of French was considerably superior to their knowledge of Latin, were guaranteed equality of access to the institutions of the state. Secondly, with French being made the sole official language, the use of 'patois' i.e. regional and/or rural language varieties, were prohibited in the official conduct of State business. Peasants and workers, most of whom were speakers of these languages varieties, had to have recourse to interpreters. In the period following the Ordinance, French became consolidated as the language of the King, the nobility and the small section of the bourgeoisie involved in the administration of the State. The Colleges, run in 18th century France by the Church, taught Latin originally, but eventually also introduced the teaching of French based on a Latin grammar and model. With the rise of capitalism in the middle and late 18th century in France, there was the resulting increase in the influence of the financial, merchant and industrial bourgeoisie. There was as well a tendency for French to spread, and for it to become unified around the variety spoken by the rising bourgeoisie. (R. Balibar et al., 1974 pp. 31-55; pp.57-80) In place of the pre-1539 diglossia involving Latin versus all the other languages used in France, the post-1539 period saw the development of a new diglossia, this time involving the ruling class variety of French, influenced by written Latin-type models, versus the language varieties used as means of informal spoken interaction among the mass of the population.

With the coming of the French Revolution in 1789, the centralised authority of the French State increased considerably. As a result, official language policy became more important than in the period of the Monarchy, and, therefore, the link between official language policy and diglossia becomes even clearer. The bourgeoisie of France, the class that seized power as a result of the revolution, was centred in and around Paris. However, members of this class also existed in the other regions of the country. Wherever this class existed, it tended to be French-speaking. Meanwhile, by the most optimistic estimates of the period, no more than a half of the population in the country could claim to be native-speakers of the population in the country could claim to be native-speakers of French. It was in these circumstances that bourgeois official language policy in France really took shape.

What can now only be interpreted as a short-term tactical concession to the various regional languages in the interest of the immediate survival of the bourgeois revolution, was made early in the period of the new regime. A decree was issued on 14th January 1790, instituting the translation of official documents into the various regional languages. This measure was taken to ensure that speakers of these languages understood the principles of the revolution and rallied to the cause at a time when it was under serious threat.

The long-term strategic intentions of the new bourgeois ruling class can be seen, however, in the steps which the authorities took subsequent to this. A second decree on language was issued on 2nd October 1790, instituting the reading of official texts in French at the end of the Sunday Mass in church, in the non-French-speaking regions of the country. This second decree, it would seem, was aimed at the compulsory exposure of the non-French-speaking population to the language which the ruling class had designated as the official language. Laws passed by the French National Convention declared, on 21st October 1793, that state-run primary schools should be set up where children would learn French. A few days later, on 26th October, the Convention further declared that only French should be used as a medium of instruction in schools. And two months later, in December 1793, the Committee for Public Safety prohibited the use of German in Alsace, and by January 1794, a decree was issued ordering the appointment in every non-French-speaking commune of a French-speaking teacher. It should be noted that the imposition of French by the post-revolutionary ruling class of France was disguised in very effective ideological trappings. The French language as the sole language of the French nation was presented as the symbol of the emerging French national identity, and as a vital medium for preserving the national unity and territorial integrity of France. (Calvet, 1973, pp. 74-75; 1974, pp. 165-166; R. Balibar et al., 1974, pp. 80-118)

The linguistic alienation of the people of France was not restricted to the non-French-speaking sectors of the population. It even extended to the French-speaking section of the population. According to R. Balibar et al. (1974, pp. 119-151), the new official form of French became codified based on the literary variety of the language. This variety was, in turn, patterned on the Latin-based models of the language previously developed and taught in the Colleges of the Ancien Régime. A simplified and modified version of this model of French, known as 'français élémentaire', was the language form to be used and taught in the primary schools. The literary variety of French was to be reserved for use in

secondary schools and at higher levels of education, as well as in the
official functioning of the State.

The general goal of the official language policy of the new French
Republic was, according to Calvet (1974, p. 173), the political and
economic domination of the people of the various regions of
France, and their assimilation into the capitalist French State. In a
more detailed discussion of the language issue, R. Balibar et al.
(1974) managed to establish convincingly that the language policies which originated with the French Revolution were aimed at, (i)
creating a common language among the new bourgeois ruling class
which could serve as a medium of ruling class inter-change at the
national level, and (ii) imposing this common language (French) on
the institutions of state such as the education system, judicial
system, etc.., which were being developed by the new ruling class,
and which were under their control. In the course of achieving these
aims, this official language policy had two effects. The first of these
was that the French language, the symbol of the rising bourgeoisie
within the new state structure, itself became more uniform and
standardised. Secondly, with the growth of the centralised bourgeois state apparatus, there developed an increased role for
Standard French as the sole official language. This served to
emphasise the diglossia between Standard French as the language
of the state versus the other language varieties in use within the
country. The diglossia involved Standard French on one hand, and
(i) colloquial varieties of French, and (ii) distinct regional languages
such as Basque, Breton, Catalan, etc., on the other. This diglossia
has lasted until the present time. Marcellesi (1979, 1980) presents
a clear and detailed discussion of diglossia in present day France.

That this process is not simply a European one, can been seen by a
quick look at the language history of Japan. In response to the
spread of Western capitalist influence in the 19th century, Japan
underwent a rapid process of 'modernization' along capitalist lines
during what is known as the Meiji period (1868-1912). During this
period feudalism was abolished, the feudal fragmentation of the
country brought to an end, and the country placed under the
effective control of a central state administration based in Tokyo.
(Schirokauer, 1978, pp. 403-443). Prior to the Meiji era, the
written form of Japanese was the *gikobuñ*, 'the imitated written
ancient language' which made use of the grammar and vocabulary
of ancient texts. In the early Meiji period, this language variety
evolved into what was called the *futsūbuñ*, 'the common written
language'. However, the gap between this written language and the
normal spoken language of the time had become so great that,
during the Meiji period, a movement was started to develop a
written language based on the spoken idiom. This movement
became known as the *geñbuñ itchiroñ*, 'the write as you speak'
movement. Out of this came a written language called *kōgobuñ*, 'the

written language in the spoken style'. (Shirô, 1967, p. 531)

Japan was, at the end of the 19th century, a country of great dialect diversity, the distribution of dialects rougly corresponding to the borders of the only recently abolished feudal domains. (Grootaers, 1967, p. 587) Thus, when 'the write as you speak' movement developed 'the written language in the spoken style', whose 'spoken style' was it based on? As one would expect, it was the 'spoken style' of the emerging Japanese capitalist class and the educated elite associated with it, mainly centred around Tokyo. The result was that the emerging centralised capitalist state in Japan not only ended up destroying an outmoded diglossia associated with its feudal past, but, like its capitalist counterparts in Europe, also created a new diglossia which served to linguistically exclude the mass of the population from participation in the new state structure.

Diglossia and Official Language Policy in the Evolution of Human Societies: A Theory

Language plays a vital role in the process of production in any society it is the medium by which production is organised and co-ordinated whenever more than one producer is involved. Language is also the medium by which the technological know-how used in production is stored and passed on to others in the production process. Thus, language is a key element in the economic base of the society. In addition, of course, language is a vital ingredient of the institutions which the society erects to maintain the prevailing social relations, and to reproduce these social relations. No government administration, religious or political institutions, could possibly function as we know them without the use of language. It is clear, therefore, that language is central to the superstructure of society, also. (Person, 1973, p. 91; E. Balibar et al., 1974, pp. 13-14; Calvet, 1974, pp. 62-63)

Diglossia involving as it does the language of the state machinery and those who control this machinery, on one hand, and the everyday language of the ordinary members of the population, on the other, serves two functions. It firstly serves to make it difficult or impossible for the ordinary members of the population to have access to, or participate in, the state institutions which have so much power over their lives. It also denies them direct access to information and technology vital to any but the most elementary forms of production. This is because, particularly in modern societies, it is centralised institutions within the state which carry out the functions of preserving and disseminating information and technological know-how. These institutions usually operate in the official language, very often in its written form. This, therefore, represents a denial of the linguistic rights of the mass of the population since they are denied the right to use the only language which they know in order to gain access to these important areas of their society. Secondly, diglossia manages, while serving the first function just discussed, to simultaneously serve another. It provides exclusive access to state institutions, as well as information and technology, for the ruling class and its functionaries. It is after all their language which is being used for the purpose of running the state institutions, as well as the storing and dissemination of information and technology.

In the 19th century, the trend towards the creation and strengthening of the nations states was a vital ingredient of the development of modern industrial capitalism. The elitist and centralised official language policies and practices which accompanied this trend, served the interests of the emerging industrial capitalist ruling classes. It gained these classes official language rights while denying these rights to be the mass of the population. There is, however, an inherent contradiction in the implementation of such language policies and practices. Modern industrial capitalism has, in the interest of its own survival, moved increasingly away from the use of direct coercion as a means of maintaing social order. It has tended, instead, towards an emphasis on the use of ideological controls. Ideological control is exerted via institutions such as the mass media, the education system, social and political organisations, etc. Meanwhile, modern industrial processes of production demand the reproduction of a literate and highly skilled labour force, as well as the expansion of this section of the general work force. And it is the same institutions used for ideological control, notably the education system, which are used to reproduce and expand the literate and skilled labour force. It should be noted that all the institutions used for the dual purposes of ideological control and reproduction of labour skills, function with the use of language, the official language. Thus, the existence of any gap between the official language and the everyday language of the mass of the population hinders rather than helps these institutions in the efficient performance of their functions. The task of those in control of these institutions would logically be to find and use the most efficient language medium(s) for communicating with the mass of the population. And here is where the contradiction lies in the official language policies and practices of modern industrial capitalist states. It involves how to devise an official language policy which would simultaneously achieve the following:

(i)   Set apart the official language from the informal everyday language of the mass population, so as to assert ruling class control and preserve privileged access to state institutions, and

(ii) Avoid the creation of too great a gap between the official language and the language behaviour of the mass of the population, in order not to hinder the state institutions in the efficient performance of their functions.

In a sense, the problem is one of how to have diglossia and yet not have it.

In Britain, a country with a long tradition of elitist and centralised official language policies, pressure is building up for a resolution of the dilemma discussed above. For example, Trudgill (1979, pp. 9-23) argues strongly in favour of the growing trend in Britain towards the toleration of regional dialects and away from the imposition through the education system of spoken Standard British English (SBE) on speakers of non-Standard British English varieties. He supports this trend as positive by stating that, in the long term, it would be simpler to change people's attitudes to non-SBE dialects than to change the linguistic habits of the majority of the British population. (Trudgill, op. cit., p. 22). He further argues (p. 23) that 'It is probably the case, though, that if in the long term, greater dialect tolerance could be achieved even in written English, children would become more articulate and enthusiastical writers' (my emphasis). This last proposal represents a clear move in the direction of bringing official language policy into line with the requirements of the employers of labour in British industry.

The logic of this position lies in the following line of reasoning. Increasing levels of skill in the written language are being required of those entering the industrial work-force. At the same time, for a large number of those entering the work-force, such skills may only be achievable in the non-Standard varieties of English which they use as their native language varieties. Society should, therefore, be prepared to tolerate written forms of these non-Standard dialects. If official language policy in Britain were to evolve in this direction, without interruption, Britain would have managed to resolve the problems which arise from the at least partial diglossia which exists between SBE, on one hand, and the non-SBE dialects spoken by the mass of the population, on the other. But this is reckoning without the pressured that would continue to exist for the maintenance of SBE in its privileged position. After all. in a society which continues to be stratified along class lines, SBE is the linguistic symbol of ruling class dominance. As well, it serves as the medium for providing privileged access to the official institutions within the society. Thus, far from there being an early resolution to the dilemma, this dilemma is likely to become more acute. The reason is that the logic of advanced industrial society will probably increase pressure for liberalisation in the area of official language policy. Meanwhile, the continued dominance of the society by the ruling class is going to mean on ongoing commitment to SBE as the official language, resulting simply in heightening of the dilemma as time goes by.

The situation in Italy provides another example of the dilemma facing official language policy in advanced industrial capitalist societies. In a situation of extreme dialect diversity, Italy has, since its establishment as a unified state in the period 1891-1870, pursued a very centralised official language policy. This has involved the sole use of Standard Italian as the official language, language of written communication and language of education. This approach to official language policy was particularly strong during the period of Fascist control in Italy.

Since the end of the Second World War and in the train of post-war industrial expansion in Italy, there has been a trend in the direction of liberalisation in the area of official language policy. This has been particularly true of the education system. In a critique of the older, normative methods of imposing Standard Italian on the population by means of the education system, Mioni et al. state, 'What in older times was recognized as "superior" norm (even if rather disputable) is now debased to a kind of deep-rooted school tradition that pushes teachers into adopting a repressive attitude towards students' spontaneous expression. This, does hinder the students from developing their expressive potential and from appropriating for themselves the means of linguistic production, in order to let their own culture come to the fore'. (Mioni et al., 1979, p. 100) The emphasis here on 'spontaneous expression' and 'expressive potential' is quite significant, and does reflect the kind of linguistic skills in the written language which are required of a significant proportion of the work-force in modern industrial societies.

Against this background, the major language-related problems in the Italian education system involve the following issues. Firstly, there is the problem of dialect interference in the written Standard Italian of speakers of non-standard dialects. And secondly, there is the problem of the poor educational performance of lower class dialect speakers in rural areas, and even more so, those who have become immigrants to the urban industrial centres. (Mioni et al., op. cit., pp. 101-102)

The solutions being proposed by a range of analysts in Italy and summarised by Mioni et al. (op. cit., p. 102), involves (i) the narrowing of the diglossia between Standard Italian and the non-standard dialects by developing '...a new Standard closer to real-life behaviour and more open to everyday usage in the various regions of Italy', and (ii) an expansion in the role and functions of the non-standard dialects within the education system. We can see, therefore, that in Italy, as in Britain, the realities of modern industrial society are creating pressure for the reform of traditional elitist official language policies. As in Britain, however, such pressure will not lead to any permanent solution. On one hand, it is true that a more liberal official language policy is likely to improve the ability of those in the work-force to manipulate written language, which is, in turn, likely to improve productivity and thus serve the interests of those who own and control capital. On the other hand, however, such liberalisation also promotes a spirit of equality and makes it easier for speakers of non-standard dialects to participate actively in official domains. This is, of course, totally against the interests of those who own and control capital. Hence the dilemma of how to have a diglossic situation and yet not have one!

Norway provides another example of a modern capitalist state trying to come to terms with the dilemma created by the existence of diglossia. A marked diglossia existed in Norway in the 19th century between the official written language. Dano-Norwegian, and the spoken language varieties of the mass of the population. The former was a language variety inherited from the period of Danish occupation of Norway, and was, in fact, as form of Danish. With the consolidationof Norway as an independent state at the beginning of the 20th century, the continued role of Dano-Norwegian as the sole written and official language was raised into question. This was done both on nationalist grounds and on the grounds that it was not a language which the majority of the population could thoroughly understand and use. Out of this grew a movement for language reform based on the principle of respect for the linguistic integrity of every individual within the state. The early language reformers, supported by the state, proposed that the New Standard Norwegian, New Norse, should be standarised with this principle in mind. New Norse, therefore, was to be firmly rooted in popular speech, and was to allow for regional variation as far as possible, without the new standard losing its coherent structure. New Norse was to serve primarily as a written language since, it was felt, writing needed to be much more standardised than the spoken language needed to be. In fact, such was the zeal to eliminate diglossia that legislation was passed which prescribed that education be carried on using local dialects. (Vikor, 1974, pp. 109-114)

This was indeed an enlightened and democratic approach to official language policy. However, Norway remained a class society dominated by the bourgeoisie. The urban bourgeoisie, speakers of Dano-Norwegian, strongly resisted the expansion in the prestige and functions of New Norse. By the 1950's, this resistance to the language reforms introduced since the turn of the century had borne fruit. The expansion in the prestige and functions of New Norse, at the expense of Dano-Norwegian, was halted and even partially reversed. The effectiveness of the resistance of the urban bourgeoisie was a result of the power which they wielded over the economy, the mass media, etc. (Vikor, 1974, pp. 109-114) All this has resulted in an interesting language situation in contemporary Norway. New Norse, a standard language closely akin to the speech of most Norwegians, functions as the official language of Norway. It co-exists alongside another de facto official language, Dano-Norwegian, the elite prestige language associated with the urban bourgeoisie. The liberal and democratic ideals of the language reformers have been partly stifled by ruling class assertion of power in the society. The co-existence of New Norse and Dano-Norwegian as official languages in Norway presents the dilemma of official language policy in advanced capitalist countries in sharp relief. The official use of New Norse represents the trend favouring the elimination of diglossia. The continued official use of Dano-Norwegian, on the other hand, represents the trend favouring the maintainance of diglossia. Norway, therefore, presents a new twist to the dilemma facing advanced capitalist countries, i.e. of how to have a diglossia and yet not have one.

Conclusion

Diglossia was the norm in pre-capitalist states such as Ancient Egypt and China. The rise of industrial capitalism and the development of the modern nation-state which usually accompanies this development, however, favours the destruction of traditional diglossias. This has been the experience of nearly all the industrialised capitalist states of Western Europe, as well as the experience of Japan. The new language situation which tends to emerge in the wake of the disappearance of an old diglossia, is one which involves a dichotomy between the official standard language variety, on one hand, and the non-standard dialects and/or minority languages, on the other.

For the poor and dispossessed, the ones who are usually not native-speakers of the new standard language variety which has emerged, a new diglossia now exists. Even though the linguistic differences between the official standard language variety and other language varieties spoken within the speech community may not be as great as that which existed traditionally, the official standard language variety does present a language barrier for many. And this is occurring in advanced industrial society which, each day, is becoming more complex, demanding increased literacy skills and higher livels of competence in the official language from those who make up the population. The language question and what, in effect, is a new diglossia, therefore, become problems which have to be faced in societies such as Britain, Italy and Norway.

The theory being put forward here is that, with the increasing technologcical and organisational complexity of human society, there exists a pressure for the elimination of diglossia. However, social inequality tends to exercise a pressure in the opposite direction. This direction is one which either leads to efforts beig made to retain an old diglossia, or where this not possible, to constitute a new one. The pressure of technological and organisational factors, however, tends to be stronger, since these factors are ones on which the continued existence of the society depends. In these circumstances, therefore, there is a continuing tendency for the gap between the official language variety and those varieties used by the mass population for everyday informal communication, to become narrower and narrower. This is achieved (i) by the assimilation or elimination of non-official language varieties as a result of the influence of the official language, and (ii) by the progressive shifting of the official standard language in the direction of the speech of the mass of the population. Of course, the merger never quite takes place in class-dominated societies. The reason is that, with every shift of the official variety in the direction of popularly used non-standard varieties, there is a reaction among the privileged classes within the society. This reaction takes the form of efforts to recreate diglossia, even if the official language variety and the popularly used varieties of language involved in this new diglossia are not as distinct, linguistically, as they would have been previously.

CHAPTER 2.

The Language Question And Socialist Transformation: An Analysis

Among the areas covered by the last chapter was the development of bourgeois official language policies in the course of bourgeois revolutions, notably the French Revolution. During the 20th century, many revolutions have occurred, several of which claim to be socialist in orientation. This chapter will examine the kind of official language policies and practices which have emerged out of these revolution, and assess the extent to which these policies and practices help or hinder in the achievement of the socialist goals set by these revolutions. The final section of this chapter, presents a sketch of what a genuine revolutionary and socialist approach to the language question should be. It is within the framework of this approach that we will, in succeeding chapters, deal with the question of official language policy in the Creole-speaking Caribbean.

The Language Question in the Soviet and Chinese Revolutions

According to the most recent available statistics, Russian is the native language of 58.6% of the population of the U.S.S.R. The other 41.4% are native-speakers of one of the approximately 129 other languages spoken within the borders of the Soviet Union. (Comrie, 1981, p. 1) At the time of the revolution in 1917, the percentage of native-speakers of Russian versus native-speakers of other languages was similar to that already cited. The Bolsheviks, on seizing power in 1917, came face to face with a very complex ethnic and linguistic situation. Under the Tsars, Russian was the sole official language for nearly the entire Russian Empire. Languages other than Russian were often repressed by the authorities, or were, at least, officially ignored. With the coming to power of the Bolsheviks under Lenin in 1917, the language question became an important element in the policies of the new revolutionary government as they related to the issue of equality and autonomy for the non-Russian nationalities. Comrie (op. cit., p. 22) outlines the major aspects of the new Soviet official language policy which emerged after the revolution, as follows:

> *First, the new state was to have no official language and this still remains true de jure for the U.S.S.R. and its constituent parts: Russian is not the or one of the official languages, nor are any of the languages of Union Republics or lower levels of autonomy. Secondly everyone was to have the right to use his own language, both in private and for public matters, such as addressing meetings, correspondence with officials, giving testimony in courts. Thirdly, everyone was to have the right to education and availability of cultural materials in his own language.*

In order to practically implement such an ambitious official language policy, during the period immediatley after the revolution, writing systems were devised for over half the languages of the U.S.S.R. Not only were all the languages with substantial numbers of speakers included, but languages such as Nivkh and Chukchi with present-day speakers numbering about 4,000 and 13,000 respectively. (Comrie, op. cit., pp. 23-24) The difficulties encountered in attempting to achieve this were, as one would expect, enormous. The new revolutionary government was undertaking such a daunting task in the early 20th century, at a time when linguistic science was relatively underdeveloped. In addition, many of the languages to be reduced to writing were previously undescribed by linguists, and, as well, were very often subject to tremendous dialect diversity. In spite of these problems, however, the literacy rate in the U.S.S.R. rose from 44.1% in 1920 to 87.4% in 1939, this marked increase including many who had acquired their literacy in languages other than Russian. (Comrie, 1981 p. 28)

All this is not to suggest, however, that the very democratic ideals surrounding official language policy after the revolution have been realised. At the time of the revolution, Russian was the native language of well over 50% of the population. It is, therefore, hardly surprising, both from a numerical standpoint and from the point of view of the traditional political dominance of the Russian-speaking population within the empire, that the Russian language would emerge as the major language of wider communication within the U.S.S.R. Russian emerged as a means of bridging the language gap which existed among the linguistically diverse peoples who made up the Soviet Union. In fact, in addition to fostering the use and development of local languages, another major aim of post-revolutionary official language policy was to promote bilingualism in Russian among the non-Russian speakers within the country. In order to help achieve this, Russian was made a compulsory subject in schools across the country. This was, of course, a practical and sensible measure aimed at promoting inter-communication among the various language groups. It is inevitable, of course that, with

Russian emerging as the major medium of wider communication across the various language groups, some element of diglossia would emerge among native-speakers of languages other than Russian. Contemporary Soviet official language policy finds itself faced with pulls in two apparently opposite directions. On one hand, there is need for the spread of competence in Russian. On the other hand, there is the long-standing commitment to the development and expansion in the functions of the whole range of languages used within the Soviet Union.

We will now examine how recent Soviet policy initiatives have attempted to come to terms with what, in my view, is a false dilemma. In late 1978, the Presidium of the U.S.S.R. Academy of Sciences met to review the question of improving the study and teaching of Russian in the national republics. According to Petr N. Fedoseev, Vice-President of the Academy, in his closing remarks to the meeting, the study and dessemination of Russian does not infringe upon national languages and cultures within the Soviet Union. One of the major focal points of his remarks was the teaching of specialised disciplines within institutions of higher education in the national republics. These disciplines had hitherto been taught, usually, in the native language. He viewed this trend as one which was progressive from a cultural and historical standpoint since it broadened the social functions of the national languages. He argued, however, that at present there was great need to train specialists from the non-Russian republics who would have a facility in the Russian language. Such specialists, according to him, would therefore find it easier working in republics other than their own. Fedoseev concludes, therefore, that the specialised disciplines which are required subjects in Soviet institutions of higher learning, should be taught in Russian. (Solchanyk, 1982, pp. 29-30) It was against the background of this kind of opinion that, in the late 1970's, the Soviet central authorities took steps to implement (i) the use of Russian as the medium of instruction for specialised disciplines in all institutions of higher learning within the country, and (ii) the teaching of Russian in all pre-school institutions. (Solchanyk, 1982, pp. 32-33)

The current trend in Soviet official language policy and practice seems to definitely conflict with the spirit of the official language policy which emerged after the Revolution. One would assume that the purpose of teaching specialised disciplines in non-Russian republics using languages other than Russian was to communicate the subject matter of these disciplines in the most efficient manner possible, i.e. via the native languages of those persons being taught. It is rather odd, therefore, that a decision would be made to teach in Russian so as to increase the level of exposure of students to Russian. This gives the impression that, for those sections of the

Soviet state structure which advocate such a position, it has become more important to expose students to the medium, Russian, than to the subject matter of the specialised disciplines. The first priority, it would seem to me, ought to be to communicate the subject matter of the disciplines which, because it was made available in local languages, would become immediately accessible to the mass of the local populations. The teaching and learning of Russian for purposes of wider communication within the USSR, important though this is, must take second place to what is obviously the priority.

As for the issue of the teaching of Russian in pre-school institutions in non-Russian parts of the USSR, what is involved is the insertion of Russian into a domain which has previously been the sole preserve of the native language. And this is being done at an age and level where the native language behaviour of the children involved has not yet been consolidated. Given the general importance of Russian within the society as a whole, this could well be interpreted as a step in the direction of wiping out the languages of those who do not speak Russian as a native language.

The direction taken by Soviet official language policy since the Revolution has been generally positive and democratic. However, several factors have increasingly come into play since 1917. The USSR has become increasingly centralised over the years. In addition, increased industrialisation coupled with advances in science and technology, have made it absolutely necessary that internal communication across the barrier of local languages be promoted. These factors have tended to push Soviet official language practice, if not policy, away from the ideals which emerged out of the Revolution.

Let us, for purposes of comparison, look at the emergence of official language policy in another major country in which a socialist revolution has taken place, i.e. the People's Republic of China. On coming to power in 1949, the new communist regime found itself confronted with massive language problems. The first of these involved the traditional Chinese diglossia, mentioned in Chapter 1, which had survived well into the 20th century. *Weu-li* or Classical Chinese had remained the basis of the official written form of the language and this was significantly different from the varieties of Chinese spoken by the people of China in the 20th century. The other major language problem involved the marked dialect diversity within the Chinese language. According to Lehmann (1975, p. 48), there are at least eight dialect groups in Chinese which differ sufficiently enough to be considered separate languages, were it not for the attitude of the speakers and the tradition of a single written language. The largest dialect group consists of Northern Chinese which accounts for 70% of all speakers of Chinese in the country.

The communist regime of 1949 was not the first government in China in this century to be confronted with these problems. From the first days of the establishment of the Nationalist Government in 1911, pressure was being exerted by some groups for a solution to the problem of diglossia. The proposed solution was to establish a form of the Peking dialect as the basis of a new official written language. (Barnes, 1973, p. 39) A campaign was launched by the May 4th Movement in 1919, advocating the use of the modern spoken language as the sole basis for written Chinese. (Lehmann, 1975, p. 42) In the 1930's, this trend towards the constitution of a modern official written language based on the Northern dialects, and more specifically the speech of contemporary Peking, was opposed by the Chinese Communist Party. In opposing a move by the Nationalist Government in the 1930's to impose modern spoken Pekinese as the basis of the official national language, the Chinese Communist Party pointed to the massive illiteracy then prevalent in the country. The position of the Party was that a major first step in the direction of national development and the creation of a true democracy, had to involve a programme for eradicating illiteracy. In the view of the Chinese communists at that time, the most effective means of doing this was via the dialects spoken by the various sections of the illiterate population. To attempt, therefore, to create a single officially used written variety of Chinese based on the dialect of Peking did not make sense. This would serve to exclude from literacy acquisition all those who were not speakers of the dialect on which the written form was to be based. (Barnes, 1973, pp. 36-37; De Francis, 1967, pp. 130-131)

The Communist Party, during the 1930's, proposed to use a Latinised writing system rather than traditional Chinese characters, as a medium for providing literacy in the various regional dialects to the large illiterate population. The Latinised writing system which the Party favoured was one called Latinxua Sin Wenzi (Latinised New Writing) developed for use in the Soviet anti-illiteracy campaign among the 100,000 ethnic Chinese in the U.S.S.R. This writing system was taken into the Communist-controlled areas within China where it received the support of many important Communist leaders. The line of the Chinese Communist Party on the question of an official language for China was that a Peking-based standard variety of Chinese would perform the role of the national common language, provided that it was not imposed on regional dialect speakers as the sole standard variety of Chinese. (Barnes, 1973, pp. 36-37; De Francis, 1967, pp. 130-131)

When the Chinese Communist Party came to power in 1949, however, they pursued a policy very similar to the one which they were opposing during the 1930's. In 1955, it became official policy to promote a single new official standard variety of Chinese,

Putonghua or 'the Common Speech'. Putonghua was to be based
on the contemporary spoken dialect of Peking, on the grammar of
the northern dialect group to which the Peking dialect itself
belongs, and on the vocabulary of modern literary Chinese. It was
the hope of the authorities that, under the new social conditions
prevailing in the period after the revolution, the vocabulary and
style of the new standard would be close to the language of the
working people in the communes and the factories. The aim was to
avoid Putonghua developing into a diglossic standard remote from
the language of everyday life. What, however, clearly indicated the
total turnabout in the language policies of the Chinese Communist
Party, was the complete repudiation of any notion of creating
separate written forms for the various varieties of Chinese. Instead,
the new standard language was to be spread around the country
vigorously, and to be used as the sole medium of education and
literacy acquisition. This had the effect of reversing what was, up to
then, the normal practice of using local dialects as the oral medium
of instruction in local schools. (Lehmann, 1975, p. 17, p. 49)

There seems to have been little documentated discussion on the
new official language policy of the Chinese Communist Party in the
post-revolutionary situation, nor on the reasons for repudiating the
old policy which dated back to the 1930's. There were, however,
faint signs of dissent concerning the fact that the new policy
seemed geared to phase the regional dialects entirely out of
existence. But here is where any public questioning of the new
official language policy seems to have stopped. The authorities
within the People's Republic of China have, nevertheless, over the
years presented some justification for the new policy. The decision
to promote Putonghua as the sole official variety of Chinese was
justified on the grounds that it would make communication across
the nation more efficient. The refusal to give any form of official
status to any of the regional varieties of Chinese was justified on the
grounds that the promotion of these language varieties would
destroy national unity. (De Francis, 1967, p. 141; Lehmann, 1975,
pp. 9-54)

One aspect of pre-revolutionary party policy which did survive in
the period after the revolution concerned the non-Chinese minority
languages spoken within the borders of the People's Republic of
China. In this perhaps emotionally less charged area of language
policy, the Chinese Communist Party was, in the period after the
revolution, able to stick to its original proposals first put forward in
1931. These proposals involved a commitment to the development
of national minority languages, in both their spoken and written
forms. According to the constitution introduced in 1954, no official
discrimination against national minorities is allowed. In the autonomous areas established for the national minorities, the respective languages are given official status alongside Chinese. All

institutions of the state in these autonomous areas use local minority languages in their dealings with the local populations, and all Han Chinese working in these areas are required to learn the local language. (Lehmann, 1975, pp. 113-114)

In both the Chinese and Soviet revolutions, there is a tendency for early position on the language question to be democratic and consistent with the view that language rights, like political and economic rights, should be made available to all. However, in both cases, a problem seems to arise at some stage in the implementation of language policy in line with original revolutionary ideals. The problem was one of praticality. A decentralised official policy cannot be implemented in a highly centralised state system. Thus, when Soviet and Chinese revolutionaries actually found themselves in power, their commitment in theory to democratic and decentralised official language policies were in total conflict with the highly centralised state structures which were being built. Official language policy, therefore, had to be modified.

The Language Question in an Ex-Colonial Society: The Case of Tanzania

With the imposition of European colonialism on countries in Asia, Africa and the Americas, came the imposition of European languages as official languages of the colonies which were created. With the coming of political independence, many of the ex-colonies retained the language of the former colonial power in the role of official language of the newly independent state. Countries as far apart as Surinam, Jamaica, Senegal and Ghana have retained the language of the former colonial power, be it French, Dutch or English, as the official language. This kind of official language policy only serves, of course, to perpetuate and re-entrench the diglossia which developed during the colonial period. The colonial diglossia involved the language(s) used by the mass of the population in informal everyday interaction, on one hand, and the official European state language, on the other. It is this kind of language situation which is being perpetuated long after the formal departure of the colonizing power.

The new post-independence ruling classes in these countries tend to have language behaviour which distinguishes them from the mass of the population. Members of the ruling classes are either diglossic themselves, operating in the local language(s) for private, informal interactions, and in the European official language for public, formal and official purposes, or they are monolingual in the official European language. The mass of the population, however, are largely monolingual in the indigenous language(s).

Several excuses are usually put forward to explain the maintenance of this kind of official language policy in the post-independence era. One of these is the need which exists for the countries to have quick and efficient access to modern science, technology and information, all of which are only immediately available in the 'international' ex-colonial languages. In reality however, such a policy only provides quick and efficient access to these areas of knowledge for members of the ruling class and those most closely associated with that class. The reason is that these are the only people within the society who speak and are literate in the official European language. At the same time, the mass of the population, who have little or no knowledge of the official 'international' language, are excluded from access to modern science, technology and information transmitted in this language.

A post-colonial official language policy which involves the retention of the ex-colonial language as the official language, has another effect, however. It serves to consolidate control of the machinery of state in the hands of the new local elite. This elite, largely the only social group able to use the official language in which the state machinery operates, ends up with a virtual monopoly control of the state.

The kind of post-colonial official language policy discussed in the previous paragraph will not take up too much of our attention here, as the elitist and undemocratic nature of such policies is pretty obvious. There is, however, another kind of official language policy. It is one which involves a decision to make an indigenous language the 'national' and official language in place of the language of the former colonial power. Algeria, India, Indonesia and Tanzania, are among the countries which have adopted this type of official language policy. The adoption of such policies usually occurs in circumstances where there is strong pressure to decolonise the society, remove the symbols of colonial domination, and assert the national identity. In fact, in the case of Algeria and Tanzania, such language policies have been accompanied by the assertion that they have been introduced as an integral element in the socialist transformation of post-colonial society. We will select for special attention the experience of Tanzania, which is fairly typical of the experiences of those countries which adopted nationalist official language policies after independence. The choice of Tanzania as the focus for the discussion is significant for another reason. Tanzania, its political, economic and even linguistic policies, have often been singled out as examples which Third World countries could do well to follow.

In the situation of post-colonial Tanzania, official language policy established Swahili as the 'national' and 'working' language of the country. The new elite who inherited state power after independence had a rather interesting view of the language situation which they had inherited. For example, Kumbo (1972, p. 39) states,

Tanzania has no less than 120 tribal languages which are all in use by their respective tribesmen. Yet as a nation, we have

*decided to adopt "Kiswahill" both as our national as well as
working language.*

Thus, while emphasising the role of Swahili as a symbol of national
unity, the post-colonial elite tries to minimize the role of the
numerous local languages spoken within the country. The use of
formerly colonial epithets such as 'tribal' and 'tribesmen' to refer to
specific local communities which possess their own particular
linguistic and cultural characteristics, is significant. For the new
ruling class, the various local languages of Tanzania represent an
obstacle to the integration of local communities into the national
economy and national political system, both of which are under the
control of this class. The same process of forced integration which
the colonial power initiated within the borders of an artifically
created state, using English and Swahili at different levels of the
system, is now being attempted by the post-colonial ruling class via
Swahili. It is, therefore, not surprising that there is some similarity
in the perspectives of the colonial and post-colonial ruling groups.
The latter group views national unity as possible only by means of
the imposition of one language, the language they wish to identify
with, on the entire country.

This policy, in addition to being in the interests of the new ruling
class, does also follow the model of official language policy
presented by the ex-colonial European powers. The official rhetoric of these European countries provides the image of a single
nation unified under one language. The reality within these
countries, however, involves the continued existence of languages
such as Welsh and Gaelic in Britain, Basque and Catalan in both
France and Spain, and, of course, the nationalism (or should we, to
be consistent, call it 'tribalism'?) associated with these language
communities. Interestingly enough, in their anxiety to bring all
sectors of the society under their control, the ruling classes of ex-
colonial countries such as Tanzania seem to conveniently ignore
the officially bi- or multi-lingual official language policies of
countries such as Switzerland, Finland, Yugoslavia, and the USSR.

Let us now briefly look at the way in which the national or
'working' language of Tanzania, Swahili, is perceived by the ruling
classes in post-colonial Tanzania. The Institute of Kiswahili
Research has been established to '... be concerned with **the study
and furtherance of the Swahili language in all its aspects, ...**'
(Prospectus of the University of Dar es Salaam, 1975-1976, p. 236)
(my emphasis) Note the focus of concern here is on the furtherance
of the interests of the **language** rather than on the furtherance of
the interests of the **speakers** of the language. Along similar lines
are a pair of statements in Kamera et al. (1976?, p. 33) which refers
to '... the main problems which face Kiswahili in its struggle to
become a truly National language ...', and to '... the possibility of

Kiswahili becoming a Pan-African language and the potentialities it possesses to stand up against the languages of "Metropoles". The narrow nationalism of the post colonial ruling class has reduced Swahili, the national or official language, to the level of a national symbol, alongside the flag and national anthem. The language therefore becomes an object whose interests, for nationalist reasons, must be promoted. This view leads, in the case of the last quote, to the idea of the 'National Language' spreading beyond the borders of the country, symbolising the spread in the influence of the nation-state with which the language is identified. Tied up with this is the notion that the 'National Language' is an object which can 'stand up' to other 'National Languages', in this case, the languages of the 'Metropoles', as part of the international struggle among nation states.

This narrow nationalism of the post-colonial ruling elites on the official language question, ignores the **function** which an official language ought to perform. The function of an official language in any country, particularly in an underdeveloped ex-colonial country such as Tanzania, ought to be involve the mass of the population in the decision-making processes of their society, as well as in its economic development. This would, of course, imply the minimum of diglossia between the language of everyday communication in local communities and the language(s) used for official purposes. Yet, in those areas of the country where Swahili is not the main medium of everyday communication among the population, diglossia is created between the local language and the sole official language, Swahili.

J. O'Barr (1976, pp. 80-84) deals with this issue in some detail. She points out that, in keeping with government policy, Swahili is the sole official language at the level of district and village councils. She notes that, at the level of the district councils where members usually come from diverse language backgrounds, the use of Swahili did serve to promote communication across language barriers. However, she argues, a knowledge of Swahili virtually becomes a prerequisite for election to district councils, thus excluding monolingual speakers of the local language.

Discrimination against non-Swahili speakers also exists at the level of the village councils. At this level, however, there is not the excuse about linguistically diverse backgrounds of participants which can be put forward in the case of the district councils. All participants at the level of village councils, according to O'Barr, tend to have a common local language as a mother tongue. However, the language used during the formal sessions of these village councils is Swahili. She observes that at village councils, women's representatives would often speak in the local language during the informal pre-meeting gatherings, but would fall silent during the formal proceedings because of their limited control of

Swahili. She also notes that old people would often come to the village councils with complaints and requests, and find themselves unable to follow the proceedings because of their limited command of Swahili. O'Barr concludes that, whereas Swahili was being used at the level of district and village councils as a symbol of national unity, its use constitutes a barrier to the active participation of monolingual non-speakers of Swahili. And such monolingual speakers generally tend to belong to the most disadvantaged sectors of the local population, notably the women, the old, and the uneducated. The major contradiction in all this, as O'Barr points out, is that this is going on in a situation where the government has officially designated the local councils, both district and village, as the main organs for instituting popular democracy and implementing its programme of socialist transformation and economic development.

Unfortunately, because of the approach of the ruling class to official language policy, the crucial complementary role which local languages should play, alongside Swahili, in the process of official communication, is apparently ignored. The problem is one of how local communities where Swahili is not widely spoken can become involved in the process of popular democracy and development when the official medium for participation in this process is Swahili only. Do members of these communities have to await their acquisition of Swahili in another generation or so before they can become involved in these processes? And in the cases of those members of local communities who speak and understand Swahili to a limited degree, but whose creative language use still rests in the local language, do their creativity and self-expression have to remain stifled by the enforced use of Swahili as the sole official language? These issues are far from being simply academic quibbles. This is illustrated by the fact that, according to Abdulaziz (1971, pp. 171-172), an estimated 10% of the Tanzanian population had had no contact with Swahili. He also states that, of the 90% who had had contact with the language, the competence of the speakers varied from those who had both Swahili and the local language as primary languages, to those in rural areas where the local language is the predominant and sometimes exclusive medium of day-to-day interaction, e.g. the rural areas of the West Lake Region, and Sukumaland.

A related issue that has to be dealt with is that of the relationship between the various varieties of Swahili within Tanzania. This is, of course, likely to be greatly influenced by the kind of approach taken to the standardisation of the language as well as the kind of decisions taken about what should constitute the accepted norm for the language. Whiteley (1968, p. 334), in discussing these issues, quotes the government appointed 'Promoter of Swahili' as stating among other things, that

*We want to rid the language of bad influences and to guide it
to grow along the proper road. We want to standarize its
orthography and usage, and to encourage all our people to learn
to speak and write properly grammatical Swahili.*

As Whiteley (p. 335) himself points out in a comment on this
statement, '... what is meant by the reference to "bad influences"
and the desire to guide the language to grow along the "proper
road"?' Harries (1968, pp. 424-429) gives us some perspective on
all this by stating that there is considerable variation in Swahili
usage between those who use the language as a mother-tongue and
those who have acquired it as a second language. As he also states,
the Swahili of those who have acquired it as a second language
would show sub-strate influences from the speakers' first language.
    The seeds of a diglossia within Swahili seem to already exist. On
one hand, there are the varieties of Swahili spoken by the mass of
the population, most often as a second language and with influence
from the first language of particular speakers. On the other hand,
there is the official variety of Swahili, to some degree an artificial
standard rooted in the written word, and the variety of the language
spoken natively by the coastal population. This incipient different-
ation can only be emphasised and further entrenched by the
intolerant view of non-standard Swahili varieties which seems to be
developing as the official position of the Tanzanian ruling elite. The
statement of the 'Promoter of Swahili' cited above certainly
expresses this kind of attitude. If such a diglossia were allowed to
develop, it would do so along class lines. There is already, on one
hand, the Swahili of the state and those who control the machinery
of state. On the other hand, there are the Swahili varieties spoken
by the mass of ordinary Tanzanians in the course of their ordinary
everyday interaction. This incipient diglossia will simply serve to
reinforce, on the level of official language policy and practice, the
class realities of post-colonial Tanzania. These realities involve the
concentration of state power and the economic power which flows
from it, into the hands of a small bureaucratic elite or 'state
bourgeoisie', to the exclusion of the mass of the population in
whose name the state is being run. (Shivji, 1976).
    Thus, the post-colonial official language policy of Tanzania has
moved in the direction of abolishing the diglossia which existed in
the colonial period between the official language, English, and the
various indigenous African languages spoken by the mass of the
population. By selecting Swahili as the sole official language in the
post-independence period, new diglossias have been created, (i)
between Swahili and the various indigenous languages spoken as
first languages by the majority of the population, and (ii) between
the official standard variety of Swahili and the various non-
standard varieties spoken by the mass of the population. That this

kind of post-colonial language situation is in no way peculiar to Tanzania can be seen by a brief discussion of Algeria. In the post-colonial period, Classical Arabic replaced French as the official language of Algeria. For the significant Berber or Kabyle minority, this constituted a diglossia between the native language of this section of the population, Berber, and Classical Arabic, the official language. Simultaneously, since the spoken language of the Arabic speaking majority was, in fact, Colloquial Algerian Arabic, the official status of Classical Arabic also created a diglossia within the Arabic-speaking section of the community. (Mansfield, 1976, p. 476, pp. 535-536).

Towards a Democratic and Decentralised Official Language Policy

The basis of an official language policy in a revolutionary situation, ought to lie in the recognition of a very important fact. The language variety spoken as the language of everyday communication by the ordinary members of a community, is the most effective language medium for releasing creativity, initiative and productivity among the members of such a community. Such a language variety is also the most effective means of promoting popular participation in, and control of, the various decision-making bodies within the state. A revolutionary official language policy would, therefore, have to be committed to the creation of a unity between the language variety or varieties used for everyday communication among the mass of the population, and the language variety or varieties used for official purposes. Such an official language policy would, by its very nature, be dedicated to the abolition of diglossia between official language and language of everyday informal interaction.

Modern centralised states tend, by their very nature, to push official language policy in a centralised and undemocratic direction. Modern technological advances have emphasised the drift in this direction, as well as have the requirements of mass communications and mass education. This trend in official language policy is based on the notion that all communication within the society emanates from the centre, from those who control the state, to the rest of the population at the periphery, who are, of course, simply passive recipients of these communications. Any programme for the revolutionary transformation of society would, of necessity, have to make entirely different assumptions about the type of communication system it would wish to create in a new society. This new communication system would have as its goal the promotion of free and efficient exchange of information, ideas, etc., between the mass of the population and those holding state power in the name of the people. An official role within the state communication system for the language varieties spoken by the mass of the population is, therefore, a must.

The question that might be quite rightly raised is that of how practical is all this. In fact, if a definite commitment is made to the principle of a democratic and decentralised official language policy, practical steps can be taken to deal with problems such as those of orthography, translation of technical terminology, and the production of adequate quantities of written material in the various local language varieties. Ironically, the same advancing technology which makes centralised and undemocratic official language practices seem increasingly necessary, also makes decentralised and democratic official language practices possible. For example, duplicators, small off-set printing machines, etc., all make community newspapers and local publications in local languages a practical proposition. Similarly, the availability of inexpensive and simple radio transmitters makes community broadcasting in local language varieties both technically and economically feasible.

In Third World countries in particular, it is easy to develop apparently left-wing and 'proletarian' objections to the kind of approach being proposed here. For many, the proposed approach is too complex, too difficult, particularly when the simple imposition of an 'international' language, usually the language of the former colonial power, seems to offer a much more immediate and easier solution. For those who favour this alternative, the imperative is for instant development, instant exposure of the population to modern science and technology. This impatience has been a vital ingredient of the official language policy of Mozambique in the period since the end of the War of Liberation. The Mozambique case, in so far as it appears to present a left-wing alternative to the kind of official language policy being proposed here, is worthy of some attention.

Hanlon (1980, p. 31) states that Portugese has been selected as the official language of Mozambique, and will be the language of commerce, government and education. He goes on to point out, however, that '... less than half the people now speak Portugese, and even then, almost always as a second language. So people are trying to learn to read a language they often speak poorly or not at all.' Hanlon is referring here specifically to the mass literacy programme launched by the Mozambican government in the period around 1979. The estimate which he gives of 'less than half the people' being able to speak Portugese is grossly over-optimistic. In the period of Portugese colonial domination, education would have been almost the only means by which the mass of the population, particularly the people in the rural areas who make up the vast bulk of the Mozambique population, could have had any exposure to the Portugese Language. But, on the admission of Hanlon (p. 31), the government of independent Mozamibque inherited from the Portugese a literacy rate of less than 15%. He goes on to state that, of this less than 15% literate section of the population, those who had as little as two years schooling made up such an important sector of the literate population that, in many districts, such persons had to be recruited a teachers in the post-independence mass literacy campaign. According to Hanlon (p. 32), many of these teachers had massive problems due to their lack of competence in the Portugese language which was being used as the medium for teaching literacy. A large number of the teachers in the literacy programme could not understand the instructions in the teachers' handbook, and many of the teachers were unable to create the discussion (in Portugese) that was supposed to be the basis of literacy instruction. In effect, therefore, of the less than 15% literates in the country at the time of independence, much less than this percentage could be said to have had an effective command of Portugese.

The above discussion suggests that the problems confronting the teaching of literacy on a mass-scale in Mozambique do not simply involve the question of how to teach the mechanical skills of reading and writing to the population. If, as is the case, the official language policy is to teach literacy in Portugese, then the language in which literacy has to be taught has to be taught also. Any understanding of the problems of language teaching would suggest that teaching people to speak a language is a much more difficult task than teaching literacy skills on their own. In addition, even when language teaching is carried out in the best of conditions, with the best of teachers and materials, the results fall far short of the active and creative skills which native speakers of a language possess. In circumstances such as those existing in Mozambique, the degree of competence in Portugese which could be acquired by the mass of the population is bound to be extremely limited. As a result, the literacy skills which they do acquire are going to be restricted by their lack of competence in the language in which those literacy skills are acquired. Thus the grave language problems not only exist, as already mentioned, in the area of teacher competence in Portugese. As well, there is the problem of a lack of knowledge of Portugese among those being taught to read and write. Hanlon (1980, p. 32) states, 'It is virtually impossible to have a discussion about words in Portugese, and each lesson must be introduced in the local language explaining what the basic sentence to be studied means.' He goes on to point out that although the Mozambique literacy programme uses Freire's method of breaking down a word into syllables and then generating new words with those syllables, this method is of relatively limited value. Students know so few words in Portugese that they cannot suggest their own Portugese examples.

A very revealing argument put forward in support of the official language policies of the Mozambique government:

> *'Freire talks of the oppressed "conquering" the language they
> speak, but which is controlled by someone else. Here (in
> Mozambique), just the opposite is true. Mozambique, not the
> oppressors, controls the language, yet few people speak it well.'
> (Hanlon, 1980, p. 32)*

If we simply ignore some of the linguistic confusions within the
positions of both Freire and Hanlon, we nevertheless notice that
Hanlon's argument is clearly contradictory. Mozambique and not
the oppressor, controls the official language, Portugese, and yet
few Mozambicans speak that official language. The real question
which is completely ignored is that of which Mozambicans speak
Portugese and which do not.

The answer to this lies in the class differentiation which
developed among Mozambicans during the colonial period, and
which continues to exist in the post-colonial situation. It is a very
tiny section of the African population of Mozambique which did
have relatively close contact with the Portugese colonizers, which
did gain access to education in Portugese, and which now make up
the bulk of the speakers of Portugese in independent Mozambique.
It is this Mozambican petty bourgeoisie which made up the bulk of
the leadership of the FRELIMO-led independence struggle, and
form the bulk of the functionaries and bureaucrats of the independent Mozambican state. It is they, not the masses, who speak
Portugese, and it is they who determine official language policy.
Their policy has had the effect of entrenching and reinforcing the
diglossia between Portugese and the various indigenous African
languages, a situation originally introduced during the period of
Portugese colonial domination.

In these circumstances, therefore, the policy of using Portugese
as the official language is going to be one which grants rights of easy
and efficient access to the institutions of state to a tiny minority of
the population, i.e. the Portugese-speaking petty bourgeoisie. And,
regardless of how great an effort is put into the spread of knowledge
of Portugese, the mass of the population, particularly the rural
peasantry who make up the bulk of the population, will be denied
right of easy and efficient access to these institutions. They will
have to acquire access via intermediaries, people who have a
knowledge of particular African languages, in addition to their
knowledge of Portugese. And, of course, it is the emerging petty
bourgeois elements who will have this combination of language
skills. There is, in effect, therefore, a channelling of mass participation in the institutions of the state via petit bourgeois intermediaries. Rather than eroding petit bourgeois power and influence within the post-colonial state, which is one of the declared
goals of FRELIMO since its accession to power, official language
policy in Mozambique is, in fact, concentrating power and influence in the hands of that class.

One of the major justifications presented for the use of Portugese as the official language is that of the role which it supposedly plays in cementing national unity.. (Hanlon, 1980; Lefanu, 1981) But one has to ask, what kind of unity? The kind of unity they are talking about is a unity of the petty bourgeoisie who are united in the fact that they all speak Portugese, regardless of the region of the country they may come from. Is the aim of the official language polity to create a unified new ruling class of petty bourgeois origin, whose power rests in the exclusive access which they have to the state apparatus? This elitist approach to the issue of language and national unity is very similar to that of the bourgeoisie in the nation states of Europe. The case of France is a notable example which we have already discussed.

The fundamentally undemocratic official language policy which emerged with bourgeois class rule after the French Revolution had an important virtue, however. It was at least providing exclusive language rights to a class which, at that period, was creative, innovative and forward-looking. Such language policies, therefore, facilitated, on the level of language, the development and expresion of creativity and innovativeness of the industrial bourgeoisie. It is this class which brought France and the rest of Europe out of the era of feudalism, revolutionising the whole area of economic production and developing it to the level at which it exists in these countries today.

The question is, what does elite rule such as could emerge in Mozambique, have to offer ex-colonial countries? According to Fanon (1963, p. 120), 'The national bourgeoisie of under-developed countries is not engaged in production, nor in invention, nor building nor labour; it is completely canalised into activities of the intermediary type.' He also states (p. 141),

> In under-developed countries . . . no true bourgeoisie exists; there is only a sort of greedy cast,, avid and voracious, with the mind of huckster . . . This get-rich-quick middle class shows itself incapable of great ideas or inventiveness.

It is elements of this class who will acquire exclusive language rights if Mozambique retains Portugese as its official language. This elitist approach to official language policy, in spite of the socialist rhetoric in which it might be clothed, simply assists in continuing the process of economic under-development endemic in ex-colonial countries such as Mozambique.

Since the petty bourgeoisie are not going to be the ones to promote economic development, the initiative for economic development will have to come from elsewhere among the population, i.e. the mass of workers and peasants. And any official language in such a situation should have the goal of ensuring that these classes of people acquire language rights. As Babu (March, 1979, p. 84) states, 'In developing countries ... where individual initiative on the part of hundreds of millions of individual (very individual) peasants is the most essential prerequisite for any kind of economic activity to take place, the denial of human rights is an obstruction to development.' The right of every citizen to have access to state institutions by means of his native language is as basic as his right to have access to these institutions. The reason, of course, is that language, whether written or spoken, is the medium by which such access is achieved. Thus, the denial of linguistic rights, as part of the overall denial of human rights, should be viewed as an obstruction to the process of economic development in Third World countries.

An approach to the formulation of an official language policy which would aid rather than obstruct the economic development and socialist transformation of Third World countries, would need to aim at achieving an important ideal. This ideal involves arriving at a situation in which the language of specific local communities, regardless of their size, is employed for the whole range of official language functions within these communities. This goal is, admittedly, an ideal, and massive problems do exist in trying to practically implement this kind of official language policy. As well such a policy will cost money to implement. However, Third World countries have to weigh the problems and costs of implementing such a policy against the problems and costs of *not* implementing it. The latter set of problems and costs involve the continued exclusion of the mass of workers and peasantry from the national system, and the continued reproduction of underdevelopment which would result from this exclusion.

In a comment which deals with the use of English as the official language in underdeveloped countries, but one which is of equal relevance to those countries which have retained French or Portugese as the official language after independence, Jernudd (1981, p. 50) states, 'The full development of local, national, and regional languages many reciprocally liberate English for use as a truly international language, a role that today is tarnished by the misuse of English to prevent the economic, sociopolitical, and cultural advancement of those who do not possess it.' This section has attempted to provide a theoretical framework within the full and democratic development of local, national and regional languages can be pursued in Third World countries.

In the following chapters, we shall use the perspective developed in these two introductory chapters as a framework within which to discuss Creole languages in the Caribbean and the role which they play or should play in the process of social and economic transformation within the region.

CHAPTER 3.

Creole Languages in The Caribbean: A Historical View

Large numbers of slaves were transported from West Africa during the 17th, 18th and 19th centuries, to work on plantations in the Caribbean. Because of the enormous area of West Africa over which these slaves were collected, there was considerable linguistic diversity among the West Africans entering plantation society. There are numerous theories about how Caribbean Creole languages developed in these conditions of language diversity, involving not only the range of West African languages but, as well, the language of the dominant European group within the colony in question. The one which I will present here is the theory which I find most logical and internally consistent. (See Bickerton, 1982, for a counter-position).

According to Alleyne (1980), in spite of the apparent linguistic diversity among the slaves arriving in the Caribbean, there was a degree of underlying linguistic unity. They all spoke languages belonging to the large Niger-Congo language family. What is more, in the earlier stages of the development of the plantation system in the Caribbean, there tended to be a concentration of West Africans who spoke languages from two closely related sub-groups within the Niger-Congo language family, i.e. Mande and Kwa. Thus, while African languages brought to the region presented a partial picture of diversity, particularly in their vocabulary and superficial syntactic features, they shared a lot in common in the area of phonology, semantics and underlying syntactic features.

Within the African slave population in the Caribbean, there quickly developed patterns of social differentiation. Thus, in-between the large mass of fiend labourers and the dominant white group, there developed an intermediate stratum made up of slaves who worked as domestic servants, artisans, slave drivers, etc. This intermediate stratu of slaves tended to have greater exposure to European language behaviour than was usually the case for the field labourers. This meant that the middle group was in a comparatively favourable position to include in their linguistic repertoire a language variety which approximated the language of the white European elite. However, it is generally accepted in the discipline of linguistics that adult native speakers of one language do not ever perfectly acquire a second language. There is always some degree of carry-over from the native language, the extent of this carry-over depending on how good the learning situation happens to be. If the learner has complete access to, and exposure to speakers of the target language, there would tend to ba a minimum of carry-over from the native language. The learning situation for the intermediate group of slaves was, however, far from ideal since they constituted a caste separate and apart from that the whites, the speakers of the European language. The access of this intermediate group of slaves to speakers of the European language, and their exposure to the language, was thus fairly limited.

As Alleyne (1980, p. 109) points, it is the vocabulary which is most often most drastically affected in a language contact situation. The new language variety which was developing among the intermediate stratum and spreading to other sectors of the slave population, therefore, tended to approximate the European language in the area of vocabulary. On the other hand, the retention of Niger-Congo language features in the syntax, phonology and semantics of the new language variety was considerable. Since the slaves belonging to the intermediate stratum and those who were field labourers ultimately belonged to the same class within plantation society, there was bound to be greater communication between these two groups than between either of these and the Europeans. The conditions were thus favourable to the spread of the newly developing language variety among the mass of Africans working as field slaves. There were other powerful factors operating in favour of its spread. It firstly provided a common and shared means of communication among Africans within the plantation system, speaking as they did many mutually unintelligible languages belonging to the Niger-Congo language family. Secondly, this new language could be learnt comparatively easily by speakers whose native language was a Niger-Congo language. The reason was that the new language variety tended to retain many of the syntactic, phonological and semantic features common to the Niger-Congo languages. The new language, therefore, had a structure which permitted a considerable amount of carry-over from the native language of speakers who had West African languages as their first language.

The above explanation helps to make us understand the reason for the strong similarity which all Caribbean Creole languages share, irrespective of whether the main source of their vocabulary is English, French, Dutch, Spanish or Portugese. The fact that Caribbean Creole languages owe their existence to the continuity of African language features under some degree of influence from European languages, has encouraged Alleyne (1980) to consider that the term 'Creole' is a misnomer, and that these languages should be more correctly referred to as 'Afro-American'. For purposes of this work, however, I will stick to the more widely used and generally accepted term 'Creole' to describe these languages.

Language and the Socio-Economic order in Caribbean Plantation Slave Society

In plantation slave society, there existed the European language (or languages). Alongside, there was the Creole language which, provided that the situation had not been disturbed by changes in the identity of the European colonising power, would have been related in vocabulary to the language of the dominant European group in the colony. In addition, there were the many, often mutually unintellible African languages of the Niger-Congo family, spoken as first languages by the large mass of slaves transported from Africa.

It was necessary in plantation slave society, like all other societies, for there to develop institutions which would protect the existing socio-economic order by promoting an ideological acceptance of the status quo among those who are oppressed by the prevailing social order. The school system, the Church and the Mass Media are all examples of such institutions, or ideological state apparatuses as we will call them. What is of great interest to us in this part of the discussion is the role of each of the languages existing in plantation slave society, in the ideological state apparatuses of the period.

In the early period in the development of plantation slave society, acceptance of the status quo by the mass of the slave population was largely induced by the use of force, i.e. the repressive state apparatus, or the threat of its use. It was only much later on that, as we will see further on, state apparatuses such as the Church started to work to induce an ideological acceptance of the socio-economic order. Forms of ideological state apparatus did exist, but these existed for the reproduction of the prevailing social relations among the dominant European groups. Slaves were thus excluded from operating within institutions such as the colonial administrative system, the legel system, and the various legislative or advisory bodies, made up as they were of the white planter class. As a result, only the language of the dominant European Group, i.e. English, French, Spanish, etc., would have been used in the functioning of these institutions. The Creole language, along with the African languages in use among the slaves, had no function in these institutions.

Since the large mass of the African slave work-force were being used for unskilled labour, there was little need for state apparatuses which would in addition to their ideological functions, reproduce labour skills. In fact, it could be argued that the aim, or at least the effect of the slave plantation system was to de-skill the African work-force. In the specific cases where there was need for skilled artisans, individual black slaves would be trained informally, using systems of apprenticeship, etc. There were, there-

fore, no institutions formally established for the reproduction of
the labour skills among the slaves, and, as such, therefore, the
question of language use in these institutions does not arise.

The Case of Haiti

The situation in Haiti during the last decade of the 18th century
largely corresponded to that described in the preceding section.
During that period, two-thirds of the slave population of Haiti were
blacks born in Africa. (James, 1963, p. 394) One could reasonably
suppose, therefore, that this two-thirds would represent the
proportion of the slave population who spoke a Niger-Congo
language as a first language. A significant and probably increasing
number of this group would have spoken Haitian French-influenced Creole as a second language. Of the one-third of the slave
population born in Haiti, one could presume that nearly all of these
would have been speakers of Creole as a first language, even though
some would have had a command of one or more Niger-Congo
languages as well.

We focus on Haiti at the end of the 18th century because it was in
this Caribbean country at this time that slavery was first brought to
an end and political independence achieved. Any attempt to
understand the language situation in the Creole-speaking societies
of the Caribbean which have recently gained their independence,
must benefit from an appreciation of what has gone on in Haiti, a
country whose independence preceded theirs by over 150 years.
The question which we need to ask concerns what role language
played in the Haitian Revolution and War of Independence. How
did language use, particularly use of Creole in the revolutionary
period as well as during and after the War of Independence, evolve
to reflect the changing socio-economic relations within Haitian
society and to reproduce those relations? And how was language
used in ideological state apparatuses such as the education system
in order to reproduce and expand the skills of the work force?

In 1791 occurred the slave uprising which led to the abolition of
slavery in what was then the French colony of St. Domingue. Haiti
declared itself an independent country in 1804. The period in
between was characterised by a struggle for power among sections
of the emerging ruling class. On one hand, there was the group of
mulattoes and blacks, many of them owners of property, who
constituted a caste of freedmen within St. Domingue slave society.
These, very often, had had some access to education. On the other
hand, there was the new black elite arising from among the mass of
the former slave population who had been liberated as a result of
the 1791 uprising. These traditionally had had little access to
education. Education in French thus became an important battleground in the struggle for dominance between the two factions.

According to James (1963, p. 175), in the period around 1796,
Sonthonax, who was the representative of Revolutionary France in
St. Domingue, set up schools where blacks were given an elementary education, and were taught Greek and Roman history. In
addition, the sons of blacks and mulattos were sent to France to be
educated in a special school set up for them by the French
Republic. The announcement by Sonthonax that no one who was
illiterate would receive a commission in the army, provided an
additional incentive for members of the emerging elite to acquire
education and, by implication, competence in French. As Honorat
(1974, p. 11) states, under the aegis of Toussaint Louvertue, there
was developing a new francophile elite made up of former freedmen, generals in the revolutionary army, and top administrative
officials and functionaries. A characteristic of this class was the
special and privileged access which its members had to education
in French.

In addition to helping to define the composition and identity of
the new ruling class, this special and privileged access to education
in French had another effect. It performed an ideological function,
operating as a symbol of the emerging French-speaking elite vis-á-
vis the mass of the population who were speakers of Creole and/or
African languages. It is quite significant that, at a period when the
mass of the black, ex-slave population was being forced back onto
the plantations to work as wage labourers, education in French was
being made available to the children of those already in positions of
privilege within the St. Domingue revolutionary leadership. The
central role which education in French was playing in the formation
of the new ruling class seems to have been recognised by the mass
of the rural agricultural labouring population. Thus, these people
begged Sonthonax, the French Republican representative, to send
them as teachers even young European children who could teach
them to read and write. (James, 1963, p. 175) This did not happen,
or if it did, it did not occur on a scale which significantly affected the
overall situation which was emerging.

The process of developing an education system operating in
French for the emerging elite of St. Domingue, was a logical
outcome of two sets of forces. The first of these was the language
policies within revolutionary France itself at this time. As we have
already seen in Chapter 1, the language policies and practices
which developed in France had two faces. On one hand, for
purposes of communicating effectively with the mass of the French
population regional languages were used to make proclamations
and decrees. On the other, however, laws were passed and steps
taken in the education system to suppress regional languages. The
aim here was to assert the dominance which the Paris-based
French-speaking bourgeoisie exercised over the entire country as a
result of the revolution.

These two aspects of the official language policy of Republican France also found expression in St. Domingue. Thus, in 1792, the proclamations of Sonthonax, a commissioner of the French Republic in St. Domingue, were issued in both French and Creole. (James, 1963, p. 175; Trouillot, 1979?, p. 9) Trouillot also refers to the fact that Sonthonax used interpreters when he needed to communicate with the black masses of the country. This aspect of the official language policy of the French Republic as it was applied in St. Domingue, can be seen by another example. A proclamation, written in Creole and dated 1801, was sent by the First Consul, Napoleon Bonaparte, to the rebellious blacks of St. Domingue, demanding their loyalty to the French Republic. (Berry, 1975, p. 92) The other aspect of official language policy within the French Republic which was extended to St. Domingue, involved the vigorous spread of French among the emerging revolutionary elite of St. Domingue. It also involved the exclusive use of French in the newly developing state apparatuses, notably the administrative bureaucracy and the education system within the colony.

The policies of the French Republic, involving as it did the promotion of French as the language of education and of the new elite in revolutionary St. Domingue, were probably not the decisive factor in shaping official language policy in that Caribbean territory. The decisive factor was the conditions prevailing at the time in St. Domingue. French was the official language of the colonial state institutions being inherited by the emerging black and mulatto elite. In addition, this was the language in which many members of this elite, particularly those who had been free before the abolition of slavery in 1793, had already acquired some literacy. As well, Creole had no standard writing system at the time and, in the absence of any steps to develop one for the language, it could not be used as a means of teaching or acquiring literacy or as a written medium for conducting government business. The continued official use of French in revolutionary St. Domingue and the spread of its use among the new elite, perfectly served the interests of this emergent ruling class. It served to ensure, as a French-speaking elite, their access to and control of the various sections of the state apparatus. Simultaneously, it served to help dissipate any illusions among the Creole-speaking black masses that they (the masses) were the true inheritors of the state and its economic base. The consolidation of a neo-colonial ruling class within the bosom of the revolution occurred rapidly, between the initial slave uprising in 1791 and the declaration of independence in 1804. Thus, according to Honorat (1974, p. 11), on the declaration of Haitian Independence in 1804, the new elite was able to use its control over the state machinery to develop an economic base for itself through the confiscation of plantations formerly owned by whites. As we have seen, language played an important though unstated role in the formation of the new ruling class in Haiti.

In 1806, Dessalines, the first head of state of independent Haiti, was assassinated. In the ensuing civil war, the Haitian state split in two. There was the northern state under Christophe, and the southern state under Pétion. The dominant ruling group which emerged in each of these two rival states could roughly be identified with the two main factions which had developed within the new Haitian ruling class. In the north, the mainly black section of the elite who had been slaves right up until the slave uprising, and who had developed into a landowning group via their positions as senior officers in the revolutionary army, were in control. In the south, the predominantly mulatto section of the elite, made up of former freedmen many of whom were traditionally owners of considerable property, were in charge. In both states, which remained separate until reunified in 1820, French continued to be the official language. However, there were stirrings within both states concerning the language question and the need to resolve some of the obvious contradictions in the area of official language policy.

In each of the two states, the particular aspect of the language issue which some attempt was made to tackle was different. In the northern state under Christophe, the focus was on the contradiction of an independent Haiti which had just thrown off the French colonial yoke retaining the language of the former colonial power as its own official language. According to De Vastey, a high official in the Christophe administration, 'Next to a change of religion, a change of language is the most powerful method of altering the character and manner of a nation. It was resolved in council ... that instruction should be given in the English tongue, and after the English method.' (De Vastey, 1823, p. 214) Christophe, in his correspondence with William Wilberforce, stated that the emergence of English as the dominant language within Haiti, in preference to French, was the sole means of preserving national independence. (Nicholls, 1979, p. 269n) There is no evidence to suggest that, in spite of the resolve to replace French with English in the role of official language, there was any significant change in the official roles and functions of French in northern Haiti. In the midst of all this concern about the symbolic importance of the official language, no attention was paid to the language of the Creole-speaking mass of the population nor to the idea that they had language rights which ought to have been protected.

In the south of Haiti, under the control of Pétion, there was some focus paid to another aspect of the language question. Trouillot (1979?, p. 9) mentions that soon after the declaration of independence, Etienne Gérin made a plea in favour of using Creole as the official language of the new nation. His plea was, of course, ignored. Gérin, probably in consultation with others holding a similar point of view, put forward the proposal that, in order to

integrate the Creole-speaking sectors of the population effectively
into the education system, Creole should be used initially. He
proposed that only when the basic skills had been imparted that a
transition to French should take place. In order to support his
proposals, he wrote a Creole grammar intended for use in the infant
classes within the schools. Unfortunately, however, Pétion paid no
attention to this project. (Brutus, 1948, pp. 62-64) In spite of the
very enlightened proposals put forward by Gérin, the rights of the
Creole-speaking mass of the population were ignored as completely in the southern part of the country as they were in the north.

There is, at present, an argument going on in Haiti as part of the
on-going Creole/French debate. The argument is about whether
Creole should have become the official language of the country
when independence was declared in 1804. A very popular position
on this question as represented by Trouillot (1979?) is that, had
Creole been adopted as the official langue, Haiti would have been
even more isolated from the outside world than it was during the
19th century. In fact, the reasons for Haiti's isolation during this
period were purely political. Haiti represented in the eyes of its
enemies an independent black country which had overthrown both
slavery and colonialism by force of arms. Thus, all other states
involved in slavery and colonialism viewed Haiti as a threat and a
dangerous precedent. Ironically, it was France which shared a
common language with the French-speaking ruling class, which was
most committd to the destruction of independent Haiti. There was
a danger of isolation embedded within the official language policy
of 19th century Haiti. With French operating as the official
language and the language of the elite in a primarily Creole-
speaking society, official language policy served to increase the
isolation already developing during this period between the ruling
class and the Creole-speaking mass peasant base. This isolation
was a factor which could only have served to weaken the ability of
the state to resist external pressure and foreign intervention.

The pre- and Post-Emancipation Periods in the rest of the Caribbean

One of the state apparatuses operating to produce ideological
acceptance of the status quo among the black population of the
Caribbean, was the Church. In the circumstances of 18th and 19th
century Caribbean, religious instruction and education in its more
general sense were synonymous. Thus, according to Gordon (1963,
p. 6), 'In the first decade after emancipation popular education was
referred to as "religious instruction"; its aims were defined, clear-
cut and well understood.' Educational skills such as literacy were
taught with the clear aim of enabling the population to read

religious literature as an element in the process of exercising
ideological control over the work-force. There was, however, no
instrumental motivation involved in the provision of this education.
The motivation for such education did not involve the need to
educate the work-force so that its productivity could increase. The
problem, whether identified as such or not, was one of how to
impart this literacy cum religious instruction to a Creole-speaking
black population.

The Danish Virgin Islands in the mid-18th century provides an
early example of this problem being tackled head on. When the
Danes took over these islands in 1755, they were faced with a
linguistic situation in which a Dutch-lexicon Creole was the
language of the vast majority of the slave population. The Moravian
Brethren and Danish Lutheran missionaries each separately created a writing system for Dutch Creole, and it was primarily through
the medium of Creole that the churches and schools set up for the
black slave population operated. Lawaetz (1980, p. 36) points out
that in the late 18th century, the slaves in the Danish Virgin Islands
had an unusually high level of literacy when compared with the
slave populations of other Caribbean plantation societies. It is
clear that the use of the language of the slave population, Dutch
Creole, as the medium through which literacy was taught, must
have contributed in some degree to the unusually high literacy rate
among the slaves of the Danish Virgin Islands. At a more profound
level, however, it is clear that the religious denominations actively
involved in the education of the slaves were deeply committed to
spreading Christianity to the black population. This commitment
lead quite naturally to both the setting up of schools and churches
for the slaves, and the adoption of Dutch Creole as the medium by
which these institutions would function. Creole within these
institutions served to ensure that the values and beliefs which the
missionaries wished to convey to the slave population, would be
passed on in the most efficient and effective language medium
possible.

Moravian involvement in the use of Creole languages as vehicles
for spreading the Christian doctrine among the black populations
of the Caribbean region, was not restricted to the Danish Virgin
Islands. An English-influenced Creole (Sranan or 'Taki-taki') was
spoken in the Dutch colony of Surinam where Dutch was, of course,
the official language. The Church in Surinam found itself confronted with the problem of how to spread its message in
circumstances where the official European language was totally
unfamiliar to the mass of the Creole-speaking black population.
The first of the Christian religious sects to conclude that Creole
was the most effective language medium for spreading the Christian gospel was the Moravian Brethren. The first Moravian
Doctrine and Catechism in Sranan were introduced in 1778. The

Moravians also translated the Bible into Sranan, and, in 1820, they produced a Sranan religious song-book. As part of their programme for reaching out to the Creole-speaking mass of the population, the Moravians, in 1832, introduced their first 'A.B.C. boekoe', aimed at introducing Sranan speakers to literacy in their own language. Use of Sranan in the Moravian Church in Surinam has become so well established that, even on to the present, Sranan remains the most important language within the Moravian Church in that country. (Voorhoeve, 1971, p. 309; Reinecke, 1975, p. 433)

One major motivation behind J.J. Thomas writing a grammar of Trinidad French-influenced Creole in 1869 was a concern for the effective spread of religious instruction among the mass of the Creole-speaking population. Thomas commented on the efforts which the Roman Catholic clergy were making to overcome this problem. They attempted to use 'pure' French in church in preference to English, the official language of the colony. He notes, however, that in spite of this attempt to move the language of the Church in the direction of that of the general population, 'The inefficiency of communicating instruction in a language only half understood, has long been perceived by the priests; . . .' (Thomas, 1969 (1869, p.v.) His 'Theory and Practice of Creole Grammar' was aimed at providing the clergy with a detailed description of Trinidad French-influenced Creole which they would have needed to use, in Thomas' view, if they were to effectively communicate with the Creole-speaking population. Thomas, however, did not limit himself to the question of Creole language use within the system of religious instruction. He was also directing his grammar at interpreters in the Law Courts. In this regard, he points out that though these interpreters were of good education, they commonly failed to provide adequate translations, particularly from Creole into English. (Thomas, 1969 (1869), p. iv) This concern about the effectiveness of communication with Creole speakers outside the confines of religious instruction, is significant. It paralleled the increase in the participation of Creole speakers in domains such as the Law Courts, a result of certain legal and civil rights granted to these people as a result of the abolition of slavery.

   This trend towards the development of a wider vision of the role of Creole languages in the Caribbean, can be seen in the case of Papiamentu in Aruba, Bonaire and Curacao. As with other Creole languages already mentioned, among the earliest attempts at using Papiamentu outside of its traditional communication functions, involved its use in the area of religion. The Roman Catholic Church was confronted with a language situation in which the mass of the slave population spoke Papiamentu, a Spanish/Portugese-influenced Creole, in a colony where the official language was Dutch. The response of the Church, and in particular the Dominican Mission, was to use Papiamentu in its activities. A large volume of religious

literature in Papiamentu was, as a result, produced during the 19th
century. Among these were translations into Papiamentu of the
Gospel of St. Matthew in 1844, and the Gospel of St. Mark in 1865.
As well, however, under the auspices of the Roman Catholic
Church, educational material of a more general and non-religious
character was also produced. One such work as an elementary
grammar of Dutch, in Papiamentu, written by Putman in 1849.
(Reinecke, 1975, p. 148) The existence of such a grammar suggests
that the teaching Dutch by means of Papiamentu was at least
contemplated if not actually implemented.

One might have expected that, after emancipation, the Creole
languages associated with the newly freed slaves would have
expanded in function as an expression of their newly acquired
rights as free people. In fact, however, official attitudes to the use
of Creole languages became quite hostile in the period after
emancipation. The colonial authorities could accept and even
approve of the specific use of Creole languages for the religious
instruction of the slave population during the period of slavery.
However, after emancipation, ex-slaves were expected to assimi-
late socially, culturally and linguistically into the European-
dominated societies in which they found themselves. If one takes
the case of Surinam, for example, the colonial authorities gave
permission to the missionaries to teach slave children to read in
Creole in 1844, and to write in it in 1856. However, in 1877,
fourteen years after the abolition of slavery in Surinam in 1863, the
very colonial authorities were to stipulate that Dutch be the *sole*
medium of instruction in schools. (Voorhoeve, 1975, p. 8) In the
case of Papiamentu, even though an attempt was made to formally
use this language in education in 1883, it was not until the late
1960's that the use of Papiamentu in the education system would
receive serious consideration from the education authorities.
(Todd-Dandaré, 1980, P. 83) As for J.J. Thomas and his efforts on
behalf of Trinidad French-influenced Creole, the declared policy of
the British colonial authorities in the post-emancipation period
was to wipe out the use of French Creole along with the other non-
English language varieties widely spoken in the island. (Gordon,
1963, p. 47)

In those colonies where English emerged as the dominant
European language alongside an English-influenced Creole, the
use of the Creole language in even as restricted an area as religious
instruction was ignored. This was the experience of countries such
as Jamaica, Barbados, Antigua, etc. The case of the Danish Virgin
Islands provides a fascinating illustration of this. In the 18th
century, Dutch was the dominant language of the white planto-
cracy, particularly in St. Thomas, and Dutch-influenced Creole
emerged as the most widespread language among the slaves. As we
have seen, in response to these linguistic conditions, Christian

missionaries took steps to provide religious instruction and reading materials in Dutch Creole. Starting in the late 18th century, an expansion in the influence of English planters based in St. Croix resulted in the emergence of English as the major European language in the Danish Virgin Islands, and English-influenced Creole as the most widely spoken Creole language amongst the slave population. Yet, when the Danish government decided to institute primary school education for slaves, it was decided that the medium of instruction should be English, not English-influenced Creole.. (Hall, 1983?, pp. 18-19) The irony is that the instructors for the proposed schools were to be German Moravian missionaries, the same group of missionaries who had previously been responsible for the extensive use of Dutch-influenced Creole in religious education among the slaves. The reasons why English-influenced Creole languages are so prone to being ignored when co-existing with English, would have to be the subject of an entirely separate discussion. It is sufficient here to note that there is a tremendous lack of awareness of the existence of Creole as a distinct language variety in such speech communities, exceeding the lack of Creole language awareness in other Caribbean Creole-speaking communities. The contemporary significance of this very strong lack of language awareness is an issue which we will examine in Chapter 5.

CHAPTER 4.

Popular Struggles and the Creole Language Question: The Contemporary Situation I.

The late 20th century is a period in which many language reforms are in the process of being introduced in the Creole-speaking Caribbean. As we have already seen in the previous chapter, when the question of expanding the roles and functions of Creole languages did arise during the 18th and 19th centuries, very few it any significant language reforms resulted. There were two reasons for this. The first was that the systems of economic production in place during this period did not, when compared with 20th century systems of production, require a work-force which was particularly skilled or literate. The second was that the struggles of the mass of the population had not yet reached a point where significant political and economic concessions could be forced out of the ruling classes. In the absence, therefore, of significant economic or political pressure in favour of a change in the linguistic status quo, proposals for language reform were never implemented.

The economic and political circumstances prevailing in the 20th century, particularly the latter half, are radically different. At the level of the production process, those who own and control capital are not satisfied with simply the reproduction of an acquiescent work-force through education. This was what was achieved in the 18th and 19th centuries through the equation between education and religious instruction. During the present century, with the increase in the use of technology at every stage of the production process, illiterate and unskilled labour has become associated with low productivity. The demand of the ruling class, therefore, is for a modern education system which would produce both an acquiscent labour force and a skilled and literate one. Althusser (1971, p. 148) sums up these two functions of a modern education system by suggesting that it involves '. . . an apprenticeship in a variety of know-how wrapped up in the massive inculcation of the ideology of the ruling class . . .'

On the political front, the mass of the Caribbean population in the 20th century find themselves in a far more favourable situation vis-á-vis the ruling classes. Many political rights have been fought for and won. In addition, national independence has been achieved or is in the process of being achieved in the bulk of the Creole-speaking Caribbean. This shift in the balance of power between the ruling classes on one hand, and the mass of workers and small farmers on the other, has had significant effects in the area of language. Even in those cases where the language question was not explicitly raised as part of the campaign for change, the shift in political balance of power has had the effect of validating and giving some degree of official recognition to the Creole language varieties spoken by the mass of the population.

This chapter will focus on some of the most obvious cases where the validation and recognition of Caribbean Creole languages have taken place. It will pay some attention to the interplay between those factors internal to the system of economic production, and those related to the assertion of political rights by the mass of the population, in the implementation of language reforms.

The Case of Haiti

From the time of the declaration of independence in Haiti in 1804, French functioned as the sole official language of the country. It was, however, not until the occupation of Haiti by United States forces between 1915 and 1934, that it was felt necessary to pass legislation declaring French to be the official language. The new constitution which was promulgated in 1918 declared French to be the official language of Haiti, and stated that the use of this language was obligatory within the administrative machinery and the judiciary. (Valdman, 1978, p. 360) This move to declare French formally as the official language has to be understood in the light of the political circumstances in which the new constitution was introduced. U.S. marines landed in Haiti in 1915, and imposed indirect American rule. As Nicholls (1979, p. 147) points out, the constitution which was adopted was totally subservient to the interests of the U.S.A. The declaration on the official status of French can, therefore, only be interpreted as a sop to the nationalist anti-American sentiment even then developing among the French-speaking Haitian elite. This elite had to be reassured that, in the face of the threatening presence of English in the society as the language of the occupying power, some shred of linguistic sovereignty at least was being preserved.

The nationalist movement which opposed the U.S. occupation was composed of a broad coalition of political forces, united mainly in their opposition to the American presence in the country. Some favoured a return to the hegemony of the mainly mulatto traditional bourgeoisie as was the status quo prior to the invasion. Others favoured the emergence of a new social order which would be more representative of the mass of the population than that which previously existed. Representative of this latter trend in the area of language was Georges Sylvain. Sylvain who was one of the founders of the anti-American nationalist movement in 1920, had gone on record as far back as 1901 as feeling that mass education had to be done by way of Creole if that education was to be effective. Sylvain died in 1925, not living to see the mass protests of 1929 which eventually led to the withdrawal of American forces in 1934. However, the trend towards an increased recognition of Creole continued during the period of national agitation and into the period after the the departure of foreign troops. During 1925, the first two detailed linguistic descriptions of Haitian Creole as a language in its own right were produced, one by Faine, the other by Comhaire-Sylvain. And, in 1939, Christian Beaulieu produced material intended to teach basic literacy and arithmetic using Creole. A pilot project which he arranged to test his approach was halted by his death in 1941. (Valdman, 1978, pp. 339-340; Berry, 1975, pp. 93-94; Reinecke, 1975, p. 226)

This burst of interest in Creole, the language of the mass of the Haitian population, coincided with and was an expression of the fierce anti-American nationalism of the period. With the departure of the Americans in 1934, the national unity imposed by the presence of a foreign invader gradually started to dissipate. The traditional and largely mulatto bourgeoisie began to reassert its control over the society, and this process reached its high point in 1941 when Elie Lescot succeeded to the presidency of Haiti. (Nicholls, 1979, pp. 166-167) Around 1940, the first phonologically based writing system for Haitian Creole was developed by Mc-Connell, a Methodist pastor of Scottish-Irish origin, and Laubach, a U.S. specialist in mass literacy. This writing system was used as a basis for launching an adult literacy campaign in Creole. This campaign, implemented by McConnell and persons associated with him, was launched in 1943 with the support of the Haitian government. According to McConnell (1957, p. 9), the President of Haiti, Elie Lescot, in fact, took a deep personal interest in the literacy programme.

The Official support given to adult literacy programmes in Creole from 1943 onwards, belongs to an entirely different tradition to the support for Creole by nationalists during and immediately after the occupation. The support of the conservative Lescot government for the use of Creole in adult literacy teaching originated in the functional approach to the language question imposed on the Haitian government during the American presence. The U.S. authorities favoured technical and vocational schools, and encouraged their setting up. The aim was to train Haitians to fill middle level posts of a semi-skilled kind, particularly in agriculture, with the object of creating favourable conditions for U.S. investment. (Nicholls, 1979, p. 147. p. 150) In 1922, therefore, the Department of Agriculture set up an education service section which assumed responsibility for schools in the rural areas. The non-traditional approach to education in these rural schools could be seen by the fact that, in 1924, the Department of Agriculture relaxed the prohibition on the use of Creole in schools, to permit the spoken use of Creole in the first four grades. (Berry, 1975, p. 95) Practical considerations about efficiency of communication with the rural mass of the population had to be given some weight in a vocational and technical approach to education such as this one. The effective spread of this kind of edcuation among the monolingual Creole-speaking rural population was seen as a necessary pre-requisite for the development of modern capitalist agriculture. Since the 1924 language reform in rural schools and the Creole literacy campaign of 1943 did not affect the overall status and prestige of French within the society, members of the traditional ruling class found it possible to co-exist with these language measures, and, in some cases, to even promote them.

As Valdman (1982, p. 147) points out, in order to facilitate the imparting of literacy skills to adult illiterates in rural districts, the McConnell-Laubach writing system sought to operate at as low a level of abstraction as possible while remaining faithful to the principle of one letter for one sound. As a result, there were many divergences from the French writing system, notably the employing of the circumflex to mark nasalised vowels and the use of the letters **w** and **y**. An autonomous writing system for Creole which deviated significantly from that of French was an anathema to the literate French-speaking elite groups within the society. The arguments against the orthography were that it represented a threat to the French cultural and linguistic heritage in Haiti. The new orthographic devices were seen as Anglo-Saxon features introduced as part of a British and American effort to ensure their own ability to read Creole. This appeal to nationalism was particularly potent at a time when Haiti had just emerged from a period of occupation by American troops. In 1946, as a result of the intense debate on the question, Pressoir, a major critic of the McConnell-Laubach system, and Faublas, the then minister of education, introduced a version of the McConnell-Laubach system featuring French-inspired representations in the areas of the orthography under dispute. These modifications did have the effect of causing the writing system to partly deviate from the principle of one letter for one sound. It, however, had the support of the privileged French-speaking sectors of the population, and came, under the name of the Faublas-Pressoir writing system, to take the place of the McConnell-Laubach orthography. The dominant groups in Haiti, while making very limited concessions in the direction of Creole, were able to bring pressure to bear to deny Creole an autonomous and maximally efficient orthography. This was all done under the guise of protecting the national linguistic heritage, in the form of the French language, from encroachment by North-American Anglo-Saxon influence.

Another way in which the French-speaking elite sought to protect the linguistic status quo was via the continued insistence that whatever language reforms did take place involving Creole, the ultimate objective should be to promote the transfer of literacy skills over to French, i.e. 'le passage au francais'. Proponents of educational reforms involving the use of Creole as the initial medium of instruction and literacy acquisition, therefore, have always been careful to stress that Creole was a bridge by means of which competence in the official language, French, could be reached. This is a true for the literacy programmes associated with the McConnell-Laubach and Faublas-Pressoir orthographies, as it is for the educational reforms of 1979. The commitment to 'le passage au francais' is expressed in a situation where it is quite obvious that the vast majority of those who are fortunate enough to have acquired literacy in their native language, will never acquire any significant degree of competence in French. Even though this expression of commitment to the notion of a transition to French has little practical educational significance, it performs a very important role in asserting ruling class dominance at the level of language. Underlying this notion is the assumption that it is the duty of the monolingual Creole-speaking mass of the population to acquire French, the official language. Acceptance of this assumption on the part of the language reformers, implies an acceptance of the linguistic status quo and the continued subordination of Creole vis-á-vis French.

In 1946, as a result of a period of popular protest, the regime of Lescot, representative as it was of the traditional and largely mulatto bourgeoisie, was thrown from power. The government of Dumarsais Estimé which emerged as a result of the crisis, was one which was strongly opposed to the traditional and largely mulatto bourgeoisie, and expressed the intention of governing in the interest of the mass of the Haitian black population. One would have expected some positive steps in the direction of promoting the status and functions of Creole. In fact, UNESCO was called in to give a report on the Haitian education system in 1947. The report which was submitted in 1949, recommended that the use of Creole in the education system be extended from Adult Literacy Campaign into the primary schools of the country. The Haitian government refused to implement this particular aspect of the UNESCO report. (Berry, 1975, p. 97) The new black middle class whom the regime of Estimé represented, did not see it in their own best interest to pursue a language policy which would have significantly attacked the linguistic status quo at that time. In any case, the regime was weak and was overthrown in a military coup in 1950.

Nicholls (1979, pp. 191-193) argues that, in this period, the largely mulatto traditional ruling class was reeling under the effects of attacks from the socialist movement and those advocating a black consciousness position. The government which emerged in 1950 headed by Paul Magloire, represented a last ditch stand by the traditional elite in the face of the relatively cautious and mild reforms instituted during the four years of the Estimé administration. The period under Magloire ended in 1956, and, in 1957, François Duvalier won the presidential elections and assumed political power in Haiti. The triumph of Duvalier marked the culmination of the efforts of the black petty bourgeoisie to seize political power from the traditional predominantly mulatto bourgeoisie. These efforts had begun back in 1946 with the election of Estimé to the presidency.

The Creole language was a central component of the authentic black Haitian national identity which Duvalier and those who shared his black consciousness position wished to promote. Thus, as far back as 1948, Duvalier in his writings stated that a vital element in the programme of educational reform which he proposed for Haiti was the introduction of the use of Creole in the primary schools. An article of the 1957 constitution gave Creole a kind of semi-official recognition. According to this article, Creole could be used in court cases and other legal proceedings in circumstances where the participants had an inadequate level of competence in French. In 1958, consistent with his position before acquiring political office, Duvalier called for a great crusade against illiteracy and presented a bill in the legislature allowing for primary school teaching in Creole. (Nicholls, 1979, p. 197, p. 227) Interestingly enough, however, in spite of the apparently favourable attitude of the regime of François Duvalier to Creole, very little on the *practical* level was done to change the official language practices of the state. The question, of course, is why this divergence between precept and practice.

In order to answer this question, we need to examine the character of the Duvalier regime itself. It was composed of members of the black petty bourgeoisie supported by henchmen drawn from the marginalised working class and from among the unemployed. The elements within the petty bourgeoisie who captured state power in 1957, attempted to use their control over the state machinery to entrench themselves economically. The ultimate objective of this ambitious section of the petty bourgeoisie was the destruction of the traditional bourgeoisie in its role as the Haitian ruling class, and the emergence of this new group as the new ruling class. In the fourteen years under the rule of François Duvalier, the position of the black petty bourgeoisie was strengthened, their control of the army and the civil service having been reinforced during the period. The political power of the traditional bourgeoisie had, as a result, diminished. In spite of this, however, little in the social or economic structure of Haiti had changed during the period. Economic power remained in the hands of the traditional bourgeoisie. (Fontaine, 1981, pp. 33-34; Nicholls, 1979, p. 236) The failure of the regime to effectively challenge the traditional ruling class at the level of economic power, provides the key to understanding their failure to implement significant language reforms.

Because many of the petty bourgeois elements who acquired political power in 1957 had low levels of competence in French, the use of Creole became, in practice, extended to many areas of political life from which it had previously been excluded. This had the effect of raising the status of Creole. Constitutional reforms in 1957 and 1964 granting some official recognition to Creole, along with legislation on Creole language use in primary education, unaccompanied as they were by any practical programme for implementation, were purely symbolic. They simply served to identify the group who were in government with a popular symbol, the language of the mass of the population. (Fontaine, 1981, pp. 36-37) No planned or systematic use of Creole within the area of government administration or the formal education system took place because the existence of the language barrier provided a convenient means of continuing to exclude the mass of the population from the political process. The only possible motivating factor for implementing genuine language reforms, therefore, would have been the existence of a programme for rapid economic change which would have required new official language practices, particularly in the education system. As we have seen, however, the regime of François Duvalier left the economic power of the traditional bourgeoisie almost entirely unchallenged.

All this began to change around 1971, just about the time of the death of Fraņois Duvalier and the accession to power of his son, Jean-Claude. It is a maxim that political power and economic power seldom remain separate for long. The years immediately prior to 1971 saw the beginnings of a rapprochement between the petty bourgeois elements who held political power and the traditional bourgeoisie who held economic power. The realisation of this rapprochement has been, perhaps, the major feature of the post-1971 period. In the view of Fontaine (1981, p. 33), the major section of the traditional bourgeoisie involved in this compromise was the industrial bourgeoisie which had emerged as dominant because of its initimate colloboration with foreign coporations, international banks and other foreign contractors and investors. The wedding of Jean-Claude Duvalier to the daughter of an important member of the Haitian capitalist class came, at the end of the 1970's, to symbolise the accomodation which had been worked among the dominant classes. It is within this political context that serious and

concerted efforts at language reform have been made during the
1970's and early 1980's.

The dominance of the industrial section of the bourgeoisie in the
new dispensation is crucial in the recent drive towards reform.
Fontaine (1981, p. 39) argues that the increasing dominance of the
industrial bourgeoisie highlights two major infrastructural problems in Haiti. The first of these is the lack of skilled personnel in
both the private and public sectors. The solution to both of these
problems lies in the education system and educational reform in
Haiti could hardly be addressed without dealing with the language
question.

Since the early 1940's, government sponsored Creole literacy
programmes for adults, mainly in the rural areas, had been
conducted with only a very modest degree of success. This, coupled
with the general failure of the formal education system resulted in
an illiteracy rate of 75.3% according to the official statistics of
1975. (Désir, 1978) Such a statistic could hardly be pleasing for
either the industrialising section of the Haitian bourgeoisie or
investors of foreign capital in the country. As a result of the new
alliances among the dominant groups which had emerged during
the 1970's, there was an upsurge in the level of official interest in
the language question, particularly insofar as it related to the
education system. The Centre Haitien d'Investigation en Sciences
Sociales (CHISS) had originally, in the period around 1972,
designed and obtained funding for a project to investigate the issue
of Creole versus French as the medium of instruction in primary
schools. It would appear, however, that 'obscure forces' blocked
the implementation of the original project. In 1974, the project was
refloated and received funding from the Inter-American Foundation. Thanks to 'the personal intervention' of President Jean-
Claude Duvalier, the project finally got under-way in October,
1974. (de Ronceray et al., 1976, p. 3) The ultimate goal of the
project was to provide the decision makers and other interested
persons with scientifically established fact concerning the language question in primary education. In a preliminary report at the
end of the first year of the experiement, it was claimed that a
teaching method employing Creole as the base language and
treating French as a foreign language was demonstrably more
effective than methods involving the monolingual use of French.
(de Ronceray et al., 1976, p. 35) Along similar lines during 1975, a
group within the Institut Pédagogique National in collaboration
with the Centre d'Education Permanente of the University of
Paris–V (René Descartes) carried out an experiment in literacy
teaching to adults in Creole. It was found that it was possible, in six
months, to learn via Creole to read, write and perform basic
operations in mathematics, provided that the content of the
teaching was sensitive to local conditions. (Bentolila, 1981, p. 121)

Closely tied up with this increase in interest concerning the role of Creole in education was a concern for developing a standard orthography for the language. In 1974, CRESH (Centre de Recherche en Sciences Humaines et Sociales) organised a seminar at which a new CRESH-sponsored orthography was proposed. This orthography involved a 'frenchification' of the already existing and widely used Faublas-Pressoir writing system. The CRESH orthography was supported by members of a mission sent by the French Ministry of Foreign Affairs to assist Haiti in a programme of reform in the area of primary education. Around 1979, ONAAC (Office National d'Alphabetisation et d'Action Communautaire) received a group of linguists from the University of Paris-V (René Descartes) sent by the French Ministry of Foreign Affairs. Their task was to provide ONAAC, a government agency involved in literacy teaching and community development, with technical support. The French team devised an orthography for Haitian Creole which attempted to avoid many of the anomalies in the established and widely used Faublas-Pressoir system. Ironically, the new writing system, referred to as the IPN orthography, re-introduced the 'Anglo-Saxon' letters so strongly rejected by the Haitian elite in their response to the McConnell-Laubach system nearly four decades earlier. (Valdman, 1982, p. 149) As we shall see, the IPN orthography was destined to play an important role in the education reforms which were about to take place in Haiti.

The Haitian government, in the late 1970's, found itself propelled by a sense of purpose and urgency which had not previously existed. The emerging alliance with the industrial bourgeoisie provided the petty bourgeois elements who controlled the state with an economic programme and direction which had been long absent. The sense of purpose and urgency was expressed in the injunction of the Minister of Education to the IPN (Institut Pédagogique National) to reject already existing educational models. According to the Minister, Raoul Pierre-Louis, the IPN ought to undertake an analysis of the Haitian school and the environment in which it operates, prior to proposing any new teaching methods. The research which followed indicated that the language of instruction was only one of the elements in the education process which had to be adapted to Haitian conditions. Teaching methodology and teaching materials also needed to be adapted. Following a cabinet reshuffle, Joseph Bernard, who became the new Minister of Education, confirmed his own commitment to the approach of his predecessor. Bernard was, in fact, responsible for implementing the far-reaching education reforms which took place in 1979. (Bentolila et al., 1981, p. 121)

The major linguistic innovation in the education reform of 1979 was that Creole would become both the medium of instruction and a subject within the curriculum during the first four years of primary school. The reform proceeds from the assumption that

since all Haitian children entering the primary schools speak
Creole and the majority are monolingual in this language, it is the
most efficient medium for teaching literacy and for presenting
basic concepts. By the end of the first two years of schooling, it was
expected that the child would be capable of communicating in
writing in his mother tongue. French would be treated as a foreign
language and taught as such. It would be taught as a subject, in its
spoken form, during the first two years of primary school. Its
written form would be introduced to the pupils only from the
beginning of the third year. In the fourth year, it was intended that
French would assume the role of medium of instruction for a large
number of subjects, particularly those of a technical nature. At the
end of the fourth year, two avenues lie open to the pupil. The first
involves vocational training in agriculture or as an artisan, with
instruction offered in both Creole and French. The second avenue
involves entry into the second cycle of primary education where,
presumably French would be the major language used. (Bentolila
et al., 1981, pp. 121-122; Gani, 1983; Valdman, 1982, pp. 145-146)

There was a considerable degree of outside involvement in the
programme of educational reform which was implemented in 1979.
The World Bank provided a loan to finance the construction of new
primary schools. This loan was also intended to cover the expendi-
ture associated with the reforms in educational practice, including,
of course, the language reform in the first four years of primary
school. On the eve of the implementation of the education
reforms, a symposium was held in August, 1979, on the introduction of Creole into the education system. This seminar was
organised by the Ministry of National Education, with the sponsor-
ship of the United States Agency for International Development
(USAID) and technical assistance from Indiana University in the
U.S.A. When one notes the involvement of the French Ministry of
Foreign Affairs via the team of linguists from the University of
Paris-V (René Descartes) in the development the new IPN Creole
orthography, one cannot but be struck by the large number of
foreign agencies involved in some way in the language issue in
Haiti. The question, of course, is why. It is the view of the World
Bank ((Noor, 1979, p. 17), that education is particularly effective in
increasing productivity, especially among the poor. Educated
farmers are more productive than undeducated ones. In Haiti
where (i) large landholdings operating within a capitalist mode of
production are predominant, (ii) these landholdings are in the main
owned by foreign companies, largely North American, and (iii) the
mineral extraction sector is also in the hands of such companies,
any increase in productivity resulting from improved educational
opportunities for the work-force, would result in increased profits
for foreign investors. (Pierre-Charles, 1972, pp. 109-114) The
involvement of the World Bank and North American institutions is

thus explained. As for the French, their involvement is part of a tactical withdrawal from a previous position which advocated the spread of French at the expense of local languages in conditions such as those of Haiti. The present-day policy, as expressed by their activities in Haiti, is one of preserving the ties of 'franco-phonie' by advocating the use of indigenous languages at the level of elementary education. French would, however, be preserved as the language of higher education and perform the role as the major medium of international communication for such countries.

The pursuit of language reform in the education system in Haiti was a project designed to further the interests of the industrial section of the Haitian bourgeoisie and their partners, foreign investors. As we have seen, the level of involvement by foreign institutions in the formulation and implementation of the new policies was very great. These circumstances contributed to the language reform being introduced in a rather high-handed manner. The reforms over-rode the objections of many, notably the educated French-speaking middle class, who had a vested interest in the continued exclusive use of French in the education system. In the true spirit of elite anti-United States nationalism dating back to the period of the occupation, many interpret the strong North American involvement in the reform as part of an American plot. According to Bentolila et al. (1981, p. 122), the view expressed in these quarters was that what was involved was a U.S. plot to gradually oust French from Haiti, with Creole playing the role of Trojan Horse disguising the introduction of English.

The language reform, implemented as the project of a narrow group of interests succeeded in alienating those who, under normal circumstances, would have been expected to support it. From 1961 onwards, private bodies, most of them affiliated to Christian denominations, had become involved with some degree of success in the teaching of literacy in Creole. In addition to making a significant contribution to literacy teaching in Creole per se, these bodies made important additions to the volume of material published in Haitian Creole, e.g. newspapers, novels, teaching materials, etc. All this material was produced in the Faublas-Pressoir writing system which was, at the time, the common and generally accepted orthography for the language. This activity in Creole was of a very mixed character. On one hand, there is the example of the Creole text on Haitian history prepared by the Protestant Literacy Committee which stated that the occupation of Haiti by the U.S. Marines in 1915 was welcomed by most Haitians, and was good for the country. (Bébel-Gisler et al., 1975, p. 32) On the other hand, an analysis of a report on the Creole literacy programme in Thomassique (Vanrompay, 1980) suggests that this programme was genuinely concerned with teaching literacy to Creole-speakers as part of an overall process of helping the oppressed to liberate themselves, albeit within a Christian religious framework. The introduction of the new IPN orthography without consulting those bodies already involved in the use of Creole in literacy teaching and publishing, and in the face of strong opposition from them, says something about the self-serving nature of the interests promoting the reform. In the eyes of those officially responsible for implementing the reform, the non-official bodies involved in the use of Creole in popular education were probably too independent and, maybe, even subversive. Ignoring such bodies ensured that they were excluded from the implementation of the reforms. In addition, courtesy of the new IPN orthography, the bulk of Creole non-government published material would have been obsolescent. With the customary lack of democracy which charcaterises the operation of the Haitian state, the authorities proceeded to implement the reform in the face of resistance from many who were in general sympathy with the principles underlying the new measures.

The introduction of Creole in the first four years of primary education as the medium of instruction and the medium of initial literacy acquisition, ran into stiff opposition among the vast majority of the population. (Vernet, 1980, p. 45) The problem which presents itself is one of understanding how a programme such as this which, on the face of its seemed designed to be benefit monolingual Creole-speakers who make up the vast majority of the population, could be opposed by its potential beneficiaries. Basically, the root of this resistance lay in the double standard which was being applied. Children of the poor and dispossessed were being required in government-run primary schools to acquire literacy in their mother tongue, Creole, while the linguistic basis for advancement within the society remained one's ability to use French. At the same time, of course, the children of the privileged minority continued to attend private schools where French remained the exclusive medium of instruction. There was a strong popular sentiment that what was sauce for the goose should also be sauce for the gander. Instead, what the bourgeois initiators of the reform intended was the minimum concession to Creole necessary in the interest of increased productivity and efficiency. As Berry (1975, p. 113) points out, the emerging trend was one of ruling class acceptance of Creole as a segregated, rural and lower class language, albeit with an orthography and some kind of semi-official status. In its role as official auxiliary language, Creole is simply a language which can be employed by organs of state when dealing with citizens who do not control the official language, French. Excluded from the higher levels of the formal education system, Creole serves purely as a medium for facilitating a transition to French for the tiny minority of the school population who survive the first four years. The initial exposure of this group to

Creole use in the formal education system would, therefore, not constitute any threat to the continued dominance of French. As for those who did not continue beyond the first four years, they would, at least, be literate in their mother tongue, Creole. Faced with ruling class ambivalence on the language question, the mass of the population have resisted the reforms, expressing a preference for traditional methods which ignore Creole and use French exclusively in education.

For as long as sections of the traditional French-speaking bourgeoisie continue to maintain economic and, by extension, political control in Haiti, for so long will linguistic oppression continue. A wave of political repression in late 1980 and early 1981 brought to an end the period of relative political liberalisation which had coincided with the introduction of the language reform. Sections of the press operating in Creole were the first and, perhaps, hardest hit victims of this repression. Announcers on Creole radio stations were arrested and beaten. This special attention from the authorities in no doubt testimony to the efficacy of the Creole language sections of the mass media in reaching the Creole-speaking mass of the population. Against this background, the views of Bébel-Gisler et al. (1975, pp. 32-33) seem quite justified. They argue that in Haiti many people support the cause of Creole in a political vacuum. As they say, to support the promotion of Creole without fighting for the mass of the population to seize power, is to mistake fowl dung for eggs, to confuse the shadow and the substance.

The Case of Aruba, Bonaire and Curacao

The range of functions of Papiamentu, the Spanish-Portugese lexicon Creole language of Aruba, Bonaire and Curacao, is probably wider than that of any other Caribbean Creole language. It, of course, is the language of private and informal everyday interaction for the vast majority of the population. In addition, however, it is the major medium of public communication in these islands. Papiamentu is the major language of the print medium. In Curacao, for example, the circulation of newspapers in Papiamentu is more than twice that of newspapers in Dutch, the official language. In the case of radio broadcasting, of the 16 radio stations in operation, only three do not broadcast in Papiamentu. These three are stations retransmitting broadcasts from overseas. Papiamentu is also the language of television broadcasting, with the proviso, however, that since the bulk of the films shown are of North American origin, English turns out to be the language most used in this medium. In the area of government, Dutch is the official language of administration. However, all forms of communication with the public take place in Papiamentu. Government decrees are published in both Dutch and Papiamentu, and those holding

political office use Papiamentu exclusively when addressing the
public. (Todd-Dandaré, 1980, Jeuda, 1983)

The education system has been a major means of protecting and
perpetuating the role of Dutch as the official language. In spite of
the very wide range of functions performed by Papiamentu, Dutch
has traditionally been the sole medium of education in Aruba,
Bonaire and Curacao. This is the case in a situation where,
according to the 1972 census, 80% of the population declared
themselves as having Papiamentu as their mother tongue, and only
8.8% declared Dutch as their mother tongue. Against this background, in Curacao, which accounts for over two-thirds of the
population of these three islands, it was found that during the late
1970's only 3 out of every 10 primary school pupils with Papiamentu as their mother tongue **never** had to repeat at least one year
in primary school. This is compared with 8 out of a possible 10
among those who had Dutch as their mother tongue. It is, therefore,
hardly surprising that the education system has become the major
battleground in which the struggle against the continued official
status of the Dutch language is being waged.

The impetus for the movement challenging the official role of
Dutch in these islands was provided by the incidents of 1969. A
radical nationalist movement had developed during the 1960's. It
published a newspaper called *Vito* and the movement eventually
took on the same name. In its initial phase, the newspaper was
published in Dutch. As the movement radicalised and sought a
base among mass of the population, particularly the working class,
the newspaper switched to publishing in Papiamentu. This change
in political and language orientation of the newspaper resulted in
an immediate increase in circulation, reaching several thousand
copies per week. The aim of the *Vito* movement was to shift the
labour movement away from strictly economic concerns. Instead,
in the view of the *Vito* movement, organised labour should be at the
fore-front of the struggle on wider political issues. The *Vito*
movement argued in favour of political independence from Holland, the need for a cultural revolution, and the granting of official
language status to Papiamentu. The links which *Vito* managed to
forge between itself and the labour movement helped to create
conditions which led to the radicalisation and unification of the
working class, particularly in Curacao. These conditions eventually
led to the events of May, 1969. A series of sympathy strikes in
solidarity with one group of workers who had struck for increased
wages, succeeded in bringing economic life in Curacao to a halt.
There was a massive demonstration and large-scale rioting, looting
and battles with the security forces. However, the economic
demands which they originally struck for, the granting of increased
wages to a certain group of workers, were met by the employers
concerned. In addition, a political demand which arose, for the

resignation of the government in view of its anti-worker stance, was also met. The government resigned and new elections were scheduled for September of the same year. (Anderson et al., 1975)

As a result of the September elections, the *Liberation Front* which represented the forces active in the rebellion of May, won three seats in the 22 seat parliament. These three seats gave the *Liberation Front* a pivotal role in determining who would constitute the new government. It eventually went into coalition with parties involved in the previous government, gaining two ministerial posts. The co-opting of political organisations claiming to represent the working class and their allies has gone on well into the 1970's, causing divisions in the formerly united labour movement and disaffection among the more militant sections of the mass movement. The co-opting of important sections of the mass movement by the establishment has led, in the wake of the events of 1969, to mild reform rather than to popular revolution. The two language related commitments which were squeezed out of the new coalition government were that (i) the Education Department would take steps to have produced within the shortest time possible an orthography for Papiamentu, and (ii) the Department would use this orthography as a basis for the eventual introduction of Papiamentu as a medium of instruction in the education system. The recommendations of the Commission of Investigation into the events of May, 1969, spell out more precisely the kind of concessions contemplated by the establishment for Papiamentu. The Commission was of the view that the introduction of Papiamentu into the basic grades of the school system would facilitate the transition from family to school. This recommendation was to be found alongside another one proposing the setting up of special education programmes for those from 'less fortunate social and cultural backgrounds'. (Anderson et al., 1975, p. 160, p. 168)

The period following May, 1969, was one of intense debate on the language question, particularly as it affected the education system. In 1969, the proposal was made that 'the Parisian method' be adopted. This was a programme of transitional bilingualism involving the use of Papiamentu in the first two years of schooling, after which a gradual shift to Dutch would take place. This method resembles very closely that which was implemented in Haiti an entire decade later. In 1970 and again in 1974, programmes were grammes were initiated for the production of educational material in Papiamentu. These programmes, however, only managed to produce a relatively small amount of teaching materials. In 1976, the Ministry of Education organised an education conference involving teachers' representatives, parents, school boards, as well as parlimentary and government officials on the question of language and the education system. As a result of this conference, a new project for the introduction of Papiamentu into the education system was launched in 1977. The government, however, seemed unaware of the size and importance of the project, allocating it an extremely inadequate sum of money for carrying out the first four ears of its operations. (Todd-Dandaré, 1979)

The introduction of Papiamentu into the education system was also beset by political problems involving the relationship between the various islands. An orthography based on the phonemic principle of one letter for one sound was proposed for Papiamentu. The Minister of Education found this orthography unacceptable. As a result, the Council of Ministers declared that each of the islands could experiment with its own provisional orthography within the schools. This compromise position suited Aruba where there is a strong feeling in favour of separation from the Netherlands Antilles, a grouping in which Curacao is the dominant member. Aruba chose an etymologically based writing system for itself, i.e. one in which the presumed Spanish/Portugese origins of words are reflected in the way they are spelt, and declared it the official orthography of that island. On the other hand, Curacao is using the phonemically based orthography, even though it has not been declared the official orthography of the island. (Todd-Dandaré, 1979, 1982)

In these circumstances, it is not surprising that up to 1982 Papiamentu had only been introduced as an official medium of education at the pre-primary or kindergarten level. Unofficially, it was also used where language problems were severe, e.g. schools in certain working class areas, and schools for the handicapped. Dutch remained the sole medium of education in all other areas of the education system. As Todd-Dandaré (1982) states, every government since 1969 has had the language question as a foremost pre-occupation. However, as he points out, none have taken the necessary steps to resolve the language problem by passing legislation which would (i) grant official status to a single Papiamentu orthography, (ii) grant official status to Papiamentu, and (iii) establish it as an official medium of instruction within the education system. Rather, as in Haiti, the focus has been on language use within the education system. Within education, there has been some toying with the notion of transitional bilingualism, though even this has not resulted in the introduction of Papiamentu into any level of the education system above that of the pre-primary schools. Meanwhile, Dutch continues to occupy its dominant place, both within the system of government administration and the education system, as the sole official language. As the impact of the popular uprising of May, 1969, has dissipated and the political organisations created during the period have become absorbed into the status quo, so the linguistic demands of the mass movement have become tied up in a maze of governmental inefficiency, and a web of petty insular nationalism. The lesson again seems to be, as is the case of Haiti, that the struggle for a truly democratic official language policy can only succeed as part of the struggle of the mass of the population for a genuinely democratic society.

The Case of Surinam

Surinam is a linguistic and ethnic mosaic. There are languages belonging to the Arawakan and Cariban language families, spoken by the Amerindians of the country. There is, as well, what is known as Sarnami Hindustani associated with the East Indian population who, along with the Creole Africans, constitute the two major ethnic groups in Surinam. Javanese is used within the minority Indonesian community, and Bush Negro Creole languages such as Saramaccan, Djuka and Aluku are employed as means of comunication within the various small communities made up of descendants of runaway slaves. The major language of Surinam is Sranan, the English-lexicon Creole language traditionally associated with the African Creole population. Sranan is a language which developed out the early contact between West African slaves and English colonists in the latter part of the 17th century. Even though the colony of Surinam was eventually ceded to the Dutch, Sranan survived as the major medium of communication among the slaves of the country. With the arrival during the post-slavery period of East Indians, Indonesians, and Chinese as indentured labourers, Sranan emerged as the lingua franca for communication between members of the various linguistic communities which then found themselves co-existing in the same society. It is estimated that between 85% and 90% of the Surinamese population are, presently, speakers of Sranan. (Voorhoeve et al., 1975, p. 11) This figure is very significant when one realises that the African Creole population among whom Sranan originally developed, constitute barely more than 30% of the population of the country. It is the role role of Sranan as the most widely spoken language in Surinam, and the nature of its co-existence with Dutch, the official language, which will concern us in this section.

The rise in the status of Sranan during the 20th century began in the 1940's. Koenders, a teacher, started almost single-handedly, a campaign in favour of the recognition of Sranan as a language equal in all respects to any other. He originally produced educational material in Sranan for a women's self-help group, *Pohama,* which was set up in 1943 to organise urban working-class Creole women. Koenders eventually became involved, from 1946 to 1956, in producing a monthly publication for *Pohama* entitled *'Foetoe-boi'* (Servant). The publication included articles written in Dutch as well as those written in Sranan. It also published Sranan poetry.

The publication was directed at African Creole working class people living in the slum areas of Paramaribo, the capital. It had as its aim to educate this group of people to be proud of their racial identity, their history, their culture and their language, Sranan. In the area of language, Koenders tried to establish by demonstration in his journal that Sranan could be used as a medium for serious discussion or beautiful poetry. (Voorhoeve et al., 1975, pp. 10-13, pp. 135-137)

Operating as he did in a period preceding the rise of the nationalist movement in Surinam, Koenders found himself isolated and pilloried by those who supported the linguistic and cultural status quo. During the early 1950's, there was a nationalist upsurge among Surinamese students studying in Holland. Many began to write original poetry in Sranan and explore the literary possibilities of their language. Out of this upsurge grew a new cultural movement known as *Wie Eegie Sanie* (Our own things). A deliberate effort was made to integrate both students and immigrant workers into the movement on an equal footing. A major focal point of the movement was the language question. *Wie Eegie Sanie* argued that Sranan was the only true national language of Surinam in that it originated within the country rather than elsewhere, unlike Dutch and many of the other languages spoken by various ethnic groups. Since Sranan already functioned as a lingua franca among the speakers of various languages, it was advocated that it be given official recognition as the national language of the country.

The aim was to unify the various *ethnic* groups behind a common cultural and linguistic identity. The major stumbling block on the question of a national language for Surinam was, however, the fact that Sranan was identified as the ethnic language of the African Creole group, even though it was a major medium of communication across the entire Surinam society. Those with a vested interest in the continued division of the Surinam society along lines of race were, therefore, able to attack the linguistic nationalism of the *Wie Eegie Sanie* movement and the cultural nationalism which accompanied it. According to this view, this was simply a move by the African Creole population to promote its own interests at the expense of other groups. (Voorhoeve, 1975, pp. 10-13, pp. 164-167, pp. 183-185)

There developed, out of the *Wie Eegie Sanie* movement, a political party, the PNR, led by Eddy Bruma, a leading Sranan poet, and other key figures in cultural movement. The PNR was set up in the late 1960's to fight for the independence of Surinam from Holland. The party had significant support among workers belonging to an important trade union federation in the country. In 1973, the government then in power, which was opposed to the idea of independence, fell as a result of a general strike and mass demonstrations. As a result of elections which followed, a new coalition government came to power with the PNR as a member. The major outcome of all this was the declaration of independence in 1975. With the coming of independence, however, nothing changed at the level of official language policy. Dutch remained the sole official language of the country.

In the post-independence period, there developed a split within the coalition government. The bone of contention was the economic policies of Bruma, in his capacity as Minister of Economic Affairs. These policies involved the introduction of import controls which were designed to protect and assist local capitalists. This alienated the the majority group within the coalition who saw their interests as being tied up with those of the foreign multi-national companies and the commercial sector involved in the import-export trade. The result of this difference in position was that the PNR under Bruma was expelled from the government. The increasing conflict between national capitalists, on one hand, and those who may be referred to as comprador bourgeois elements within the government, led the former group to contemplate steps which could result in a change of government. The coup which eventually over-threw the Surinam government in 1980 was planned as far back as 1978 by elements favouring the national capitalists. (Hira, 1983, pp. 177-185)

The military coup led by Bouterse in 1980, although inspired by the national capitalist section of the ruling class, occurred in the context of popular agitation within the armed forces. There had been a campaign within the army for the recognition of a union representing soldiers and non-commissioned officers. This resulted in a confrontation between the pro-union elements in the army and the Surinam government, leading to the court-martialling of prominent members of the military union. This action by the government created a groundswell of popular support in favour of the demands of the soldiers and against the policies of the government, not only as they affected the soldiers, but the mass of the population as well. According to Hira (1983, pp. 184-185), in the absence of an organised mass-based political movement to present a revolutionary challenge to the regime, the army unionists found that they had no option but to go along with the coup planned by national capitalist elements. In the view of this analysis, the national capitalists were, in fact, forced to press ahead with their own coup in order to pre-empt what they imagined would be an even more radical overthrow of the regime at some later date. The National Military Council (NMC) which was set up attempted to maintain some kind of balance between the two political tendencies within the military. However, effective political control remained in the hands of the supporters of the national capitalists. This control was demonstrated by the degree of influence which

Eddy Bruma and the PNR had on the NMC in the period after the coup. There was, as well, the temporary imprisonment of the more left-wing members of the NMC, and the various steps taken by it to suppress independent mass-based political activity within Surinam society. As Hira (1983, p. 189) points out, although the military coup was directed at the traditional comprador bourgeoisie, it excluded the involvement of the mass of the Surinam population. In order to mobilise popular support for the new regime, the newly dominant national capitalist class sought to advocate class and race harmony across the various groups which make up Surinam society. Nationalism was appealed to, with Sranan playing an important role as a symbol of the Surinam national identity.

Caught between the genuine popular upswing in support for Sranan inspired by *Wie Eegie Sanie* and others, on one hand, and the demagogic requirements of a regime dominated by the national capitalists of the country, on the other, Sranan rapidly spread into a range of official functions. At the level of international relations, Sranan made its appearance during a visit by the head of the National Military Council, Deysi Bouterse, to Grenada. An interpreter was available for translating from Dutch into English. However, Bouterse opted to address his Grenadian hosts in Sranan rather than Dutch, with his Minister of Foreign Affairs translating into English for the benefit of the Grenadians. (Eersel, 1982, pp. 3-4) As Eersel goes on to point out, the use of Sranan spread, since the military take-over in February, 1980, from simply being a language used for political campaigning to a language used by the political leadership in totally formal and official circumstances. Thus, in launching a national movement in December, 1983, Bouterse spoke entirely in Sranan except for the part of his speech in which he attacked the policies of the Dutch government. For this, he used Dutch since, according to him, he wished the journalists from Holland to fully understand what he said. In spite of the de facto use of Sranan in a range of official circumstances, no government declaration has been made concerning the official recognition of Sranan. For as long as Sranan is identified as the ethnic language of the African Creole population of Surinam, such a declaration would carry with it the danger of racial dissension.

Despite the differences in detail between the language situations of Haiti, the ABC islands and Surinam, the politics of the language situation of the latter country appears to have followed a similar trend to that of the other two. A bascially democratic process in favour of widening the range of official functions performed by the language of the mass of the population, has become coopted by a section of the ruling class in the furtherance of its own interests. In Surinam, as elsewhere, the pursuit of democratic official language policies in the absence of political control by the mass of the population in whose name reforms are implemented, leads to the manipulation of the population rather than to any advantage for them.

St. Lucia and Dominica

In both St. Lucia and Dominica, a French-lexicon Creole is the language of informal everyday communication for the vast majority. English is and has been the official language ever since the British finally seized control of these islands nearly two centuries ago. One important difference in the language situations of these two countries is the existence in Dominica of a significant English-lexicon Creole-speaking minority.

Right up until the present, language has played an important role in the continued exclusion of the mass of the population from effectively controlling power in these societies. A vivid example of this is provided by Carrington (1981). He points to the fact that the cultivation of bananas is carried out by large numbers of farmers in rural St. Lucia. Yet, according to the Saint Lucia Banana Growers Association Act of 1967, the office of delegate or other member of the Managing Committee of a District Branch cannot be held by anyone who '. . . is unable to speak, and . . . to read the English language with a degree of proficiency sufficient to enable him to take an active part in the proceedings of the Managing Committee'. (cited in Carrington, 1981, p. 1) An analysis of this regulation is important since, as Carrington (p. 5) himself points out, it serves, right down to the local district level, to exclude the majority of the potential members of the association from participating in management decisions. The regulation was based on the assumptions (i) that since English was the sole official language of the country, it would be the sole language spoken at meetings, and (ii) that, with English being the sole medium in which literacy was taught in the education system, this language would be the only medium of written communication within the association.

The level of functional illiteracy in the population over 15 years old in 1970 has been estimated by Carrington (1981, p. 4) to be 64%, with even higher concentrations of the functionally illiterate in the rural areas. Carrington goes on to point out the close correlation which exists in St. Lucia between the incidence of illiteracy and lack of competence in English. The extreme discrimination on grounds of language faced by the vast majority of banana growers in St. Lucia is symbolic of the wider discriminatin faced by the Creole-speaking populations within the society as a whole. In this regard, Jules (1979) particularly mentions the miscarriages of justice in the law courts because many defendants fail to claim the interpreters they are entitled to use. This failure is a result of embarrassment on the part of these defendants to admit publicly that they have a low level of competence in English, the official language of the country.

Dominica and St. Lucia achieved their political independence from Britain in 1978 and 1979 respectively. The language question was never raised as a political issue in the events leading up to the granting of independence. In spite of little more than a condescending recognition on the official level of Creole as a quaint archaic aspect of national life, notably a Creole motto on the Dominican coat-of-arms, a profound change in public attitude to Creole was taking place during the 1970's. This change was taking place as part of a general rise in nationalism and cultural cnsciousness. Kadans, an indigenous Dominican popular music form spread in popularity. The language of Kadans was Creole. With this music being played on radio stations in Dominica and St. Lucia, it tended to act as a stimulus for the development of Creole language broadcasts on a medium which was formerly exclusively the preserve of English. (Jules, 1979; Magloire, 1982, pp. 14-16) The broadcast of Creole programmes increased quite rapidly. Thus, as Magloire states with reference to Dominica, regular Creole language programming started in 1975, one hour per week. By 1981, approximately eight hours per week, out of a total 101½ broadcasts hours, were allocated to Creole language programmes. Use of Creole on the radio has helped, in its turn, to strengthen the popular and nationalist sentiments which originally created the conditions in which Creole could be used on the radio.

One of the effects of this general rise in national and popular consciousness during the 1970's was an adult literacy programme started by the Folk Research Centre of St. Lucia in 1975. This programme, carried out as it was among prisoners and rural inhabitants, very soon found itself confronted with the language problem. The problem was particularly acute because of the approach to literacy instruction which was adopted. According to Fr. Patrick Anthony, director of the Folk Research Centre which undertook the programme, the method of teaching involved Freire's 'conscientisation' approach, i.e. literacy was taught as part of a process making the learner more aware of the society in which he lives, the oppressive socio-economic conditions which, among other things, causes him to be illiterate, and the ways in which he can transform his society. As Fr. Anthony points out, such a method is inherently political. The problem was that, at the start, this literacy programme did not question the linguistic assumptions which pervaded St. Lucian society, i.e. that English, as the sole written and official language of the country, was the only appropriate medium through which literacy could be acquired. Yet, most of the participants in the programme were monolingual Creole speakers. As a result, the insistence of the personnel of the

Folk Research Centre on using English in the literacy classes to the exclusion of Creole, created a serious contradition within a literacy programme which was committed to the idea of following the mass of the population to 'speak their own word'. Ironically, the people being served by the literacy programme were in total agreement with the approach to language use in literacy classes which was adopted by the Folk Research Centre. The view was that there was no point in acquiring literacy in Creole since such literacy would offer neither opportunity for social and economic advancement, nor access to reading and writing skills in a language variety which was officially recognised and used.

Recognising the dilemma which faced the literacy programme in St. Lucia, Fr. Anthony states that within the Freire approach there was no consideration given to the question of the language which should be used as the medium of literacy acquisition. The reason, as he states, is that the method was pioneered in monolingual communities in Brazil in which the language question, therefore, did not arise. In spite of the enlightened attitudes of the initiators of the literacy programme, it was possible for them to simply regard Creole as an unwritten non-standard language associated with the culture of the folk, having no role to play in a context such as that of literacy instruction. The linguistic realities of the literacy programme radically changed this view. The participation in the programme of Creole speakers who spoke no English pointed in only one direction, towards the adoption of Creole as a medium of for teaching literacy. In addition to the difficulty involving the non-existence of a standard writing system for Creole, there was the negative attitude of the Creole-speakers themselves to the use of their language in the literacy proces. This resistance on the part of those persons who, in theory at least, stood to benefit the most from a change in the medium of literacy instruction, forced the Folk Research Centre to take a position on the broader question of language policy within the society at large. The Folk Research Centre was eventually pushed into the position of arguing that (i) St. Lucia was a bilingual country in which two languages, Creole and English, were in use, and (ii) the government should grant official status and functions to Creole, as well as, is presently the case, to English. It was only if this last condition was met that Creole-speakers could find literacy instruction in their native language useful and relevant. Its involvement in the activity of spreading literacy to the poorest and most dispossessed sectors of St. Lucian society, forced the Folk Research Centre to strongly advocate an increase in the status and functions of St. Lucian Creole. (Lerestan, 1981, pp. 4-5, interview with Fr. P. Anthony)

As was the case in Haiti, and to a lesser extent, Aruba, Bonaire and Curacao, the St. Lucian government did not come to grips with

the language question as a result of any concern for the social and
political enfranchisement of the mass of the population. Rather, it
was the enormous inefficiency of the education system, and the fact
that such inefficiency was seen by those who controlled the society
as a barrier to modernisation and economic expansion, which
evoked the first official government response on the Creole
language question in St. Lucia. In 1974, the government of St.
Lucia appointed a committee on educational priorities made up of
private citizens and public officers having an interest or an
involvement in education. Even though this committee did not
finally report until February, 1980, interim submissions were made
to the government in 1978, as well as drafts of the final report. The
committee recognised the need to eliminate illiteracy and felt that
Creole should play a central role in this process. In addition, the
position was taken that Creole should be used extensively within
the school system. The favourable view taken by the committee of
the use of Creole in education was a response to the difficulties
which monolingual Creole-speakers were having in the officially
English-medium education system. In mid-1979, only a few
months after independence, a new left-wing government, that of
the St. Lucia Labour Party, was voted into office. The Ministry of
Education and Culture in the new government, based on the
interim submissions of the education priorities committee, set up a
new committee in October, 1979. This committee was to specifically address the literacy question in the country, particularly as it
related to the language issue, and to report on the feasibility of
setting up a mass literacy programme. (Carrington, 1981, pp. 7-9;
1982, pp. 4-8; Seminar, 1981, p. 1)

The setting up of the literacy committee represented a con-
vergence between governmental and non-governmental attempts
to come to terms with the illiteracy problem and, by extension, the
language problem. The objective of eliminating illiteracy was part
of the election manifesto of the St. Lucia Labour Party which won
the election. As Fr. Anthony of the Folk Reserch Centre points out,
some people who now held office shared a common ideological
outlook with those involved in unofficial adult literacy activities. It
is, therefore, not surprising that, apart from the participation of
Lawrence Carrington in his capacity as a linguist with some interest
in St. Lucian Creole, the major elements making up the literacy
committee were the representatives of the Folk Research Centre
and the Caribbean Research Centre, non-governmental organisations concerned with the problems of mass education. The report
of the committee favoured a bilingual official language policy, both
in the society at large and within the education system. It was
recommended that the government supported efforts to develop a
standard orthography for St. Lucian Creole, and that such an
orthography receive official recognition when developed. In the

meanwhile, during the early part of 1980, the government initiated a national consultation on education involving a broad cross-section of St. Lucian society. The proposals which came out of this consultation strongly favoured a bilingual official language policy. They recommended a government supported programme of Creole language standardisation in order to make such a policy possible.

Arising out of the recommendations of both the literacy committee and the national consultation on education, two practical measures were initiated to tackle the language issue and the related literacy problem. The first of these was the organisation of a seminar on an orthography for St. Lucian Creole. Under the auspices of the Folk Research Centre and the Caribbean Research Centre, participants selected for their linguistic or other professional skills and/or their intimate involvement as field workers in the language situation, met together with three linguists to develop an orthography for the language. The meeting took place with financial assistance from the Ministry of Education and Culture, among others. The other measure was the governmental approval for the establishment of a National Literacy Council contained in the budget address of the St. Lucian Prime Minister in April, 1981. The budget was, however, defeated, not because of the policies which it contained, but because of the failure of the Prime Minister to secure the votes of members sitting on his own side of the house. This was an expression of a growing factionalism within the St. Lucia Labour Party government which not only blocked the setting up of the National Literacy Council but led to other serious setbacks in the move to gain official status for Creole. The internal party strife led to the resignation of the Minister of Education and Culture, Kenny Anthony whose commitment to confronting the language and related education problems had been responsible for the rapid progress which had been made in this area between 1979 and 1981. In the period of political uncertainty created by the party split, progress on the language question ground to a halt. This period of uncertainty ended with the early elections of May, 1982. The result was a victory for the political party which had held power up until 1979. This party had not traditionally been particularly interested in dealing with the language related problems of the society, and, therefore, its return to power marked a new stage in the fight for official recognition of the language rights of Creole speakers in St. Lucia. (Carrington, 1981, pp. 7-9; 1982, pp. 4-12; Seminar, 1981, pp. 1-3; Lerestan, 1981, pp. 4-5)

Arising out of the seminar on an orthography for St. Lucian Creole held in January, 1981, the Standing Committee on Creole Studies (S.C.C.S.) was formed. In May of the same year, the International Conference on Creole Studies was held in St. Lucia. This conference was attended by two delegates who, no doubt

inspired by the developments in St. Lucia, were active in the
formation of a S.C.C.S. in Dominica in June, 1981. At a workshop
held the following month in Dominica, P. Louisy, one of the persons
active in the St. Lucian S.C.C.S., presented the orthography agreed
on for St. Lucian Creole and suggested that a similar one could be
adopted for Dominican Creole. The St. Lucian orthography was, in
fact, accepted with a few slight modifications, and presented to the
public in September of the same year. Thus, while progress on the
language question was slowing down in St. Lucia, the example of
what had been achieved served to inspire fresh activity in Dominica. The irony of all this is that the government in power in
Dominica could not, by any stretch of the imagination, be described
as being committed to radical political and social change. The
Dominican government has, however, through the Cultural Division of the Ministry of Education, encouraged the annual Creole
Day or Jou Kwéyol which began to be celebrated in 1980. The
object of this celebration is to encourage Dominicans to use Creole
in as many situations as possible on that day, resulting in the
extension of Creole use to government offices, schools and other
domains where English is normally the sole language used. The
Dominican S.C.C.S. operates from within the same Cultural
Division. In addition, it was the Permanent Secretary in the
Ministry of Education and Culture who opened the July, 1981
workshop on the question of an orthography for Dominican Creole.
(Faria, 1982, p. 2; Magloire, 1982, pp. 35-43)

It should be noted, however, that the nature of the commitment
expressed by the Dominican government on the language question
is of a limited sort. It stops well short of granting official status to
Creole or integrating it into an adult literacy programme and the
formal education system. The government which came into power
in St. Lucia in 1982 followed a similar path to that adopted by the
Dominican government. While taking no active measures to
suppress the various Creole-related activities and institutions
started during the time of the previous regime, no measures have
been taken to change the official status of the language, or to use it
in adult literacy or the formal education system. The fact that
neither government, in spite of what might be considered to be its
natural inclinations, can actively oppose the pro-Creole movement,
is a sign of the growing consciousness of the mass of the population,
at both the political and linguistic levels. The fight has to continue
for concessions to be made to the rights of Creole speakers in the
areas of official language use. In the meantime, in both these
countries, the work of raising the language consciousness of Creole-
speakers continues. One medium is the monthly newspaper
Balata, published in English and Creole by the Creole committees
of both St. Lucia and Dominica. Another area of this kind of activity

involves the continuation of the annual Jou Kwéyol or Creole Day celebrations and their extension to St. Lucia in 1983.

Guadeloupe

Guadeloupe, along with Martinique and (French) Guyane, continue to be tied to the colonial power, France. They have the status of overseas departments of the metropolitian country. As overseas departments, the countries are treated supposedly as integral parts of France at the legal, political and administrative levels. It is against this status that various anti-colonialist elements have been struggling. Since the late 1960's and early 1970's, there has been a powerful upsurge in nationalist and anti-colonial sentiment in Guadeloupe. This has been accompanied by strong feelings favouring the promotion and the granting of official status to the French-lexicon Creole spoken in Guadeloupe and shared with the neighbouring island of Martinique as well as with Dominica and St. Lucia. It should be pointed out that the anti-colonialist movement in Guadeloupe is far from homogeneous in terms of the objectives. Some adherents, like the Communist Party of Guadeloupe (P.C.G) want greater autonomy for the country within the French Republic. Others see the primary goal as the achievement of national independence, and yet others perceive national independence as simply a step in the direction of creating a socialist society under the control of the workers and peasants. This range of opinion reflects itself, as we shall see later, in the way in which the various elements view the present and future role and functions of Guadeloupean Creole.

Sections of the anti-colonialist movement in Guadeloupe have, at various times, been involved in trade union activity, the organisation of various forms of public protest, and in political mobilisation among the mass of the population, as a means of pressing their demands. Since the beginning of the 1980's, the movement has entered a new phase with the bombing of various targets associated with the French colonial presence in the country. These acts of sabotage have been linked to clandestine organisations such as G.L.A. (Groupe de Libération Armée) and A.R.C. (Alliance Revolutionnaire Caraîbe). What may be emerging in Guadeloupe is the first protracted struggle for national independence in the Creole speaking Caribbean during the 20th century, in which the organised use of armed force on the part of the anticolonialists has played a major role. The only situation which bears comparison is that of the Haitian war of independence at the end of the 18th century. However, at that time, the lack of scientific linguistic information about Creole and, more importantly, the ultimate betrayal of the aspirations of the mass of the Haitian population, served to stifle any serious attempt to deal with the Creole language question. As for the kinds of language reforms currently taking place in countries such as Haiti, Curacao, Surinam and St. Lucia, these are being introduced in circumstances where there is a singular absence of the kinds of political and socio-economic changes which could provide support and reinforcement for these reforms. As a result, as we have seen in previous sections, these reforms run the risk of being manipulated, distorted and co-opted by an unjust social order. The potentially far-reaching changes which could come about as a result of Guadeloupe gaining its independence as a result of a war of national liberation, would provide favourable conditions for the introduction of language reforms favourable to the Creole-speaking mass of the population. It is this which makes the situation which is emerging in Guadeloupe particularly worthy of our attention.

The contemporary nationalist movement in Guadeloupe can trace its origins back to the formation of G.O.N.G. (Groupe d'Organisation Nationale de la Guadeloupe) in the mid-1960's. The organisation was set up with the aim of mobilising the mass of the Guadeloupean people against colonial oppression and in favour of national independence. When construction workers went on strike in May, 1967, they received the support of G.O.N.G. In the ensuing mass demonstrations and the repressions by the colonial authorities, 49 people were killed and dozens injured. The leadership of G.O.N.G., as well as many others associated with the anti-colonial movement, were imprisoned. An important characteristic of the ferment of this period was that it was restricted to the two major urban centres, firstly breaking out in Basse-Terre, and then on a much larger scale in Point-á-Pitre. Apart from the urban working class, the other significant group active in the protest movement was the nationalist intellectuals. One should, in my view, bear the composition of the movement in mind when one notes the fact that the Creole language question does not seem to have been raised.

In the period following 1967, through the long incarcerations, court trials, etc., a new direction seems to have been emerged within the nationalist movement. There was the formation of the U.T.A. (Union des Travailleurs Agricoles), a union representing agricultural workers, in 1970. This was followed by the establishment in 1972 of the U.P.G. (Union des Paysans Pauvres de la Guadeloupe) to represent small farmers. The view seems to have emerged that the rural population, particularly the agricultural workers and the small farmers, held the key to the ultimate liberation of the country. The pro-independence elements who were prominent in the formation of these organisations came to view sections of the urban working class with suspicion, perceiving them as constituting a kind of labour aristocracy with their relatively high wages and favourable working conditions. According to this view, such workers tended to be in favour of maintaining links with France since that was the only way in which their economic advantages could be maintained. This opinion is echoed by the Guadeloupean Communist Party and its union, the C.G.T., which represents this category of worker. These organisations favour autonomy but not full independence. (U.T.A., 1983, pp. 1984-1985)

This emphasis on mobilisation among the mass of the rural population had far-reaching effects on the role, status and functions of Creole within the overall political struggle within Gradeloupe. During the sugar workers' strikes of 1970 and 1975, for example, the militants of the U.T.A. employed Creole consciously and deliberately as a medium for organising the workers. In contrast to the stituation which tended to prevail with traditional unions, workers felt free to participate actively in union meetings, having been liberated from the feeling that they had to use French when they spoke publicly. The union leadership itself addressed mass meetings in Creole. The U.T.A. leadership, however, went well beyond the simple question of whether to use Creole. They were equally concerned about the style of political discourse. There was a rejection of a French-influenced style of discourse which would simply have involved Creole translations of speeches which would previously have been delivered in French. Rather, there was a preference for styles of oral communication inherited from traditional folk culture and the church. In speeches, therefore, leaders of the U.T.A. tended to illustrate rather than define, provide a parable rather than articulate a theory. The effect of this unorthodox pattern of language behaviour on the rural population of Guadeloupe was electric, which many people who attended public meetings simply being excited by the fact that their language was being used in public formal situations for the first time in their experience. (Bébel-Gisler et al., 1975, pp. 33-34, 132-135; Bébel-Gisler, 1983, pp. 2018-2021)

The challenge of the U.T.A. to the prevailing political and socio-economic system of Guadeloupe was not restricted to the local concerns of agricultural workers concerning their wages and conditions of work. The activities of the U.T.A. were part of a wider movement to challenge the power which French capitalism had over the lives of ordinary Guadeloupeans. At the national level, the attack on the linguistic hegemony of French took forms such as the refusal of U.T.A. members appearing before the courts to use French, and their insistence on addressing the court in Creole, much to the irritation of the judges. The struggles of the agricultural workers between 1970 and 1975, attracted a great deal of attention and public sympathy. Thus, Father Céleste, a Guadeloupean Roman Catholic priest working in one of the sugar-cane areas, took positions supporting the striking sugar workers in 1971

and 1975, going on hunger strike in solidarity with the workers on
the second occasion. The linguistic practices of Father Céleste
soon began to parallel those of the rural agricultural movement
with which he identified. The communiqués issued by Céleste
during his hunger strike in 1975 involved the, at least, partial use of
Creole. In addition, he began to celebrate mass in Creole from
1972. He adamantly refused to compromise with some sections of
public opinion by preaching in a mixture of Creole and French. In
his view, any such a practice would perpetuate the subordinate role
of Creole within the society. (Bébel-Gisler et al., 1975, p. 119;
Bébel-Gisler, 1983, p. 2022; Céleste, 1983, pp. 1954-1955)

The shift in political strategy on the part of the Guadeloupean
nationalist movement since the late 1960's, has remarkably transformed not only the political balance of forces within the country,
but the linguistic situation as well. The new focus on mobilisation
within the rural areas created the conditions for the raising of the
Creole language question as an integral element in the process of
national liberation. Against the background of these favourable
conditions created by the changing political situation, it became
possible for other concerned people with specialised skills to
become involved and to advance the cause of Creole further. Thus,
by 1976, G.E.R.E.C. (Groupe d'Etudes et de Recherches en
Espace Créolophone), composed of linguists and others with some
specialised interest in language, was formed and had brought out
its first issue of its publication *Espace Créole*. Members of
G.E.R.E.C., notably Jean Bernabé, developed and promoted a
phonemically based orthography suitable for Guadeloupean Creole as well as for the Creoles of Martinique and Guyane. At the time
when this proposed orthography was made public, there was
already a considerable pressure, within nationalist circles at least,
for the use of Creole in writing. Political slogans on walls in favour
of the movement tended to be in Creole. Communiqués from
sections of the anti-colonialist movement very often began and
ended with Creole slogans, even though the body of the text was
written in French. However, writing Creole, before the coming of
the G.E.R.E.C. system, involved the use of an etymological French
orthography. This orthography was inconsistent and totally unsuit-
able for the language. Thus, writing and reading Creole written in
this manner was labourious and time consuming. There was,
therefore, a pressure on those wishing to communicate in an
efficient manner, to restrict the use of written Creole to formulaic
devices such as slogans. However, the development of the phonemically based G.E.R.E.C. orthography seems to have removed the
technical barrier to the wider use of Creole in writing. By 1981. this
new orthography appears to have been accepted and adopted by
the whole of that section of the society that favoured the use of
Creole as a written language. The orthography has become the

medium by which Creole is represented on placards, political posters and banners, and in the nationalist print media such as Jougwa *(Journal Guadeloupeen)* and Magwa *(Magazine Guadeloupeen)*. In these publications, French remains the major language used. However, there is usually a section written exclusively in Creole and efforts are being made to gradually expand the role of Creole across the entire magazine. Political writing has also been produced in Creole, using the new orthography. In addition, there has been a remarkable outpouring of creative writing in Creole, also employing the orthography. The G.E.R.E.C. orthography seems to have opened the floodgates to writing in Guadeloupean Creole.

The arrival in power in France of François Mitterand and the French Socialist Party in May, 1981, radically altered the political environment in which the language question was being raised. The new government came to power on a platform which promised regionalisation, i.e. the devolution of administrative and other powers to the various regions within France, including, of course, overseas departments such as Guadeloupe. The independence movement has viewed the various moves of the Socialist government of France in the direction of decentralisation for Guadeloupe as a purely cosmetic change to the face of colonialism. (UPLG, 1982, pp. 1961-1966) One of the off-shoots of the regionalisation policies of the French government, has been a willingness to recognise the existence of regional languages within the French Republic and to allow their limited use within the education system. The Deixonne law, introduced just after the Second World War, which provides the legal basis for present government policy, does not recognise Creole as one of the regional languages of the Republic. The Socialist government of France has, however, shown some willingness to consider treating Creole as a regional language. The eagerness of the representatives of the new French Minister of Education to concede the official use of Creole in the education systems of the French overseas departments in the Caribbean, severely embarrassed sections of local public opinion instilled with the doctrine that Creole had no separate existence as a language. Apart from the exigencies of politics within the French Republic, there were certain very local realities which were also pushing in the direction of the official integration of Creole into the education system. The rate of failure in the school systems of Guadeloupe, Martinique and Guyane were three to four times that prevailing in metropolitan France. Many local educators blamed the lack of use of Creole in the education system as the major contributing factor. (Prudent, 1983a, p. 2077)

It was against this background that a group of teachers at a secondary school in the rural town of Capesterre Belle Eau in Guadeloupe, managed to persuade the school authorities to allow for classes in reading and writing Creole within the regular school timetable during the academic year 1981-82. Pupils were allotted a single half-hour class per week. The orthography employed was that of G.E.R.E.C. The whole exercise became a focus of public attention and debate, with known anti-independence elements allegedly actively involved in organising parents against the experiment. The teachers involved in the programme responded by, among other things, presenting a live class for broadcast on television. This exercise could be viewed in two ways. The view expressed by Zandronis (1981, p. 27) was that it constituted a preemptive move on the part of Guadeloupean educators to avoid the French educational and linguistic establishment co-opting the idea of using written Creole within the educational system. Were such an approach to be integrated into the colonial education system, the fear was that this would have involved the introduction of an orthography for Creole which was as close to that of French as possible. In addition, it was felt that such an introduction of Creole into the education system would have occurred in a manner totally outside the control of Creole speakers themselves. The other way in which the exercise could be viewed, as expressed, for example, by Bébel-Gisler (1983, pp. 2023-2024), was that the very acceptance by the authorities of such a proposal was part of the change in policy of the French government in the period after May, 1981. As a result, token recognition of the existence of Creole as a regional language within the French Republic could succeed in maintaining the language in a subordinate position to French. According to this line of argument, regionalisation and decentralisation within the colonial embrace of France can only signal a change in the strategy being employed to continue denying the existence of Guadeloupe as a separate national, cultural and linguistic entity. The Capesterre experiment could, therefore, be serving rather than challenging the prevailing colonial order. In my view, there is an element of truth in both positions. What is, however, quite clear is that, as of May, 1981, Guadeloupean Creole which had previously been promoted as a weapon in the struggle for national liberation, had also become a prize over which competing social and political forces were fighting.

An illustration of the growing importance of Creole as a symbol capable of manipulation by even the most right-wing forces in Guadeloupe, can be seen in the use to which the language was put during the anti-Dominican riots of 1979 and 1981. A wealthy Guadeloupean white, Viviés, was considered in nationalist circles to have played a key role in inciting crowds to lynch immigrants from nearby Dominica. A poem in Creole was distributed as a pamphlet by the henchmen of Viviès, according to reports. This poem extolled the virtues of Guadeloupeans and attempted to blame all the evils of Guadeloupean society on the Dominican immigrants. The irony in all this is that Dominicans and Guadeloupeans speak varieties of Lesser Antillean French-lexicon Creole which are extremely similar to each other. The fact that right-wing colonialist elements should feel themselves obliged to resort to the use of written Creole in their efforts to mobilise the mass of the population, is significant. A great change has taken place in the role and functions of Guadeloupean Creole since the pro-independence elements made the first step in the early 1970's. The pamphlet was written in what Hurbon (1983, p. 1995) describes as an etymological writing system or 'petit nègre'. The description of the writing system as 'petit nègre' reflects the sensitivity of the nationalist movement to anything which questions the autonomy of Creole or which seems to suggest that Creole is a bastardised form of French. Whether the writers of this pamphlet were conscious of what they were doing or not, the choice of an etymological orthography had further significance in addition to emphasising the link between Creole and French. This choice of orthography served to separate the way that Guadeloupean Creole was being written from the orthography selected for Dominican and St. Lucian French-lexicon Creoles. This latter orthography had been selected as part of a process which had involved a representative of G.E.R.E.C., Jean Bernabé. The outcome was an orthography which resembled that which G.E.R.E.C. developed for Martiniquan, Guadeloupean and Guyane Creoles in nearly every important respect. Thus, while the anti-colonialist movement was attempting to use language as a means of forging links with nearby Caribbean countries, the pro-colonialist elements were manipulating it to increase the separation between Guadeloupe and its neighbours, thus emphasising the need for continued reliance on links with France.

The manipulation of Creole is not the exclusive preserve of colonialism and its supporters, as we shall see. The change in the government of France in 1981, had an important effect in areas other than those of language. For example, the policies of the new government broke the monopoly which the French government had over radio broadcasting. It allowed the setting up of non-government radio broadcasting facilities. The anti-colonialist movement in Guadeloupe took full advantage of this relaxation in government policy. Radyo Inité, associated with supporters of the clandestine organisation G.L.A. and later on with the M.P.G.I. (Mouvement Populaire pour la Guadeloupe Indépendante), as well as Radyo Tanbou, associated with another wing of the independence movement, soon began to broadcast. These broadcasts tended to be predominantly in Creole. Creole has now made its appearance on an entirely new medium of mass communication. As the nationalist struggle has built up between 1981 and 1984, there have been many attacks by the colonial state and its supporters against the anti-colonial radio stations as well as against the anti-colonial movement as a whole. In the polarised atmosphere which has been developing, conditions have become quote favourable to various forms of ultra-nationalist deviation. This is no more true than in the area of language.

As far back as 1976, Bernabé, a member of G.E.R.E.C., argued in favour of 'maximal deviance' from French in the use of Creole for non-traditional functions. His position, as represented by Prudent (1983b, p. 38), was originally put forward in order to counter the language behaviour of certain trade union and political activists who felt that by simply creolising the phonology of their French and inserting some Creole syntactic structures, they were talking Creole. Bernabé was particularly opposed to the wholesale retention of marxist terminology borrowed from French in the supposedly Creole speech of these persons. Unfortunately, instead of defining the new norm which he was aspiring to in positive terms, as involving maximal correspondence with the everyday speech of the mass of the population, he defines it in negative terms involving the maximum degree of distance from French. The latter definition of what is desirable mistakes the nationalist shadow for the substance. The whole purpose of national liberation is to allow the mass of the local population to participate in and have control over the running of their own society. At the level of language, this should express itself by the promotion of a variety of Creole most familiar to the mass of the population. As Prudent (1983b, p. 38) argues, the principle of 'maximal deviance', when applied in an extreme way, can lead to purism and a separation from the linguistic practices of the mass of speakers of the language. This is a deviation which the nationalist parties in Guadeloupe have to be particularly wary of, especially in their role as sponsors of widely listened to Creole-medium radio broadcasting stations.

CHAPTER 5.

Popular Struggles and the Creole Language Question: The Contemporary Situation II.

In the preceding chapter, we looked at some of the more obvious cases in the Caribbean in which the Creole language question has been a burning social and political issue. It is our contention, however, that even when the language question is not raised in any explicit manner, social and political conflict in the area of language is nevertheless present. In fact, the absence of any open debate on the language question is itself an expression of the complete control which those who benefit from the linguistic status quo have over the minds of the population at large.

We here focus on the English-lexicon Creole languages such as Jamaican, Barbadian, Guyanese, Antiguan, etc., spoken in countries which were formerly British possessions, and in which English continues to function as the official language. In these societies, it is often argued that no language problem exists. These Creole languages are, after all, only 'dialects' of English. According to this view, genuine language differences only exist when there is a marked difference in vocabulary. In addition, there are usually intermediate varieties which exist between the local standard variety of English, on one hand, and the most conservative and rural varieties of Creole, on the other. Many people, as a result, find it difficult to regard such Creoles as separate languages in their own right.

The fact that many of these societies have been politically independent for some time, and share common approaches to the language question, allow us to treat them together. They in fact provide excellent examples of neo-colonial language policies in action.

Introduction

Unlike the prevailing situations in the French possessions of Martinique, Guadeloupe and Guyane, the language question was never an important issue in the anti-colonial struggles which took place in the Commonwealth Caribbean. This is particularly true of those countries in which the Creole language derives the bulk of its vocabulary from English. Within the anti-colonialist movement, the few who displayed any form of language consciousness at all, viewed Creole as simply another of the unfortunate by-products of colonialism. According to this position, the use of 'broken forms of English', i.e. English-lexicon Creole languages, would cease in the post-colonial period as a result of the exposure of the mass of the population to 'proper English'. This was to be achieved by way of an improved education system, increased access to written material and information in English, etc.

There is, however, an important set of exceptions to the above statements. This set of exceptions involves people often identified as folklorists or proponents of the folk culture. People like Louise Bennett of Jamaica and Wordsworth McAndrew of Guyana came, over a period of time, to take positions favouring the preservation of the Creole languages of their respective countries. The position which they developed was that Creole was and is a vital element in the national identity. They have proceeded to support this view by producing and publicly performing literary works in Creole. They have, as well, been involved in researching and popularising many aspects of the local culture, notably folk tales and folk songs. All this began in the period before political independence was attained, and in the face of considerable opposition from the dominant groups within the society and their spokesmen. This kind of opposition forced people like Bennett and McAndrew to take a rather defensive position on the Creole language question. They ended up stressing the need for the **preservation** of Creole in its existing roles and functions. There was, at least, a tacit acceptance on their part that, in spite of the expressiveness and efficiency of Creole as a medium of communication, the role of English as the sole official language could not be challenged. This defensive position made it easy, after independence, for the new political elite who had inherited political power, to co-opt the work and positions of people like Bennett and McAndrew. In the quest for national symbols to place alongside those of the flag and national anthem, the new political elite occasionally finds it necessary to refer to the special place with the 'folk' speek plays as a mark of national identity. But, at best, when the existence of Creole is at all recognised by those who now hold political power, this recognition is granted to a symbol and nothing more.

On the attainment of political independence, English became the sole official language of the countries of the Commonwealth Caribbean. The diglossia involving Creole as the language of everyday informal interaction for the mass of the population, and English as the written, public-formal, and official language, continued. The new political elite, with a command of English not possessed by the Creole-speaking mass of the population, were and continue to be the beneficiaries of the prevailing official language policies. The new flag and the new national anthem signalled, for the monolingual Creole-speaking majority of the population, the continued denial of their language rights. Nevertheless, the growing self-confidence of the mass of the Creole-speaking population, coupled with the need for them to be integrated within the national economy, has forced a series of **de facto** changes in language practice at the public and formal levels. This has set the stage for the gradual erosion and decay of official language policy and practice in the post-colonial Commonwealth Caribbean. It is this process which we will analyse in the following sections.

The Legal System

The question of Creole languages and the law is not one which has received any official attention in those Commonwealth Caribbean societies where English-lexicon Creoles are spoken. The general consensus among legal practitioners as well as the population at large is that English is the language of the law, and that Creole speakers can be presumed to be speakers of English. However, since a language gap does exist between the official language of the Court and the language competence of most people who come into contact with it, Creole speakers are bound to be discriminated against on grounds of language.

A glaring form of this discrimination involves a disrepsect for the language of Creole-speakers who appear before the Court coupled with an inability or refusal to understand on the part of the court officials. This is well illustrated in the Guyana example cited below.

> 'Magistrate: "What about the cursing; you didn't curse?"
> Eileen: "Yes Sir, I **is** curse"
> Magistrate: "I **is** curse?"
> Eileen: "Yes, Sir, I **is** curse"
> She was fined $15 for cursing.'
> (*Evening Post,* 7th August, 1970, cited in Yansen, 1975, p.53)

The form **'is'** so frequently appearing in the above example is, in fact, **iz,** a reduction of the habitual marker **doz.** Thus, the defendant, in response to the Magistrate's initial question, is stating that she is someone who curses. Such as response suggests that she did not understand the question, which was about whether she had cursed on the particular occasion being dealt with by the Court. The Magistrate's second question, echoing the defendant's own response, can be interpreted in one of two ways. Either he understood and was mocking the defendant's speech, or was

genuinely puzzled by the answer. In either case, however, the
defendant was found guilty and punished without her own statement being taken into account. Her statemeng was ignored in this
case because it was not presented in English, the official language
of the Court.

In many other situations, however, the Court is forced to
recognise the existence of Creole, albeit in a piecemeal and **ad hoc**
manner. A newspaper article entitled 'Tell the court what happened then' (*Guyana Daily Chronicle*, 10th September, 1982)
sheds some light on Creole language use in court. The article refers
to the fact that Creole is often used in the Court since its use serves
the double function of saving time and ensuring clarity. In fact, in
the opinion of the writer of the article, this use of Creole in the
Guyana courts has been on the increase. As the article points out,
lawyers and even magistrates are forced to resort to the use of
Creole with witnesses who fail to understand questions addressed
to them in English. The article also refers to the case of a defendant
who did not understood when the magistrate asked him to plead
guilty or not guilty. It was the prosecutor who intervened to provide
a Creole translation. It is usually at some juncture in the court
proceedings where it is necessary for a monolingual Creole speaker
to answer a question or provide the Court with information, that
some form of translation into Creole is resorted to. And the role of
unofficial interpreter is carried out by anyone in the Court carrying
out official functions who feels that he can make himself under--
stood to the Creole speaker concerned.

Contrast the above to the attitude of the Courts to speakers of
language varieties clearly identified by the society and the Courts
alike as being **not English.** Any monolingual speaker of a language
such as Dutch, French or Spanish is provided with an official Court-
appointed interpreter whose job it is to (i) translate into the
native language of the speaker questions asked of him by the
Court, (ii) translate the responses of the speaker into English for
the benefit of the Court, and (iii) if the speaker is a defendant,
translating for him the proceedings of the Court. Monolingual
Creole speakers suffer greatly by comparison. The magistrate or
judge, one of the lawyers, or maybe a Court-reporter, emerges as an
ad hoc Creole interpreter for questions addressed to such monolingual speakers. Translations of responses in Creole are not
usually made since the assumption is that all present in Court have
at least a passive competence in Creole. However, it is not always
certain, in my view, whether persons with the social and linguistic
backgrounds of lawyers, magistrates and judges, are always able to
make precise and exact interpretations of Creole utterances. And,
of course, exactness and precision in the interpretation of what is
said is of the essence in legal proceedings. A further disadvantage
faced by a monolingual Creole speaker who is a defendant, is the

fact that there is no official Court-appointed interpreter or anyone else for that matter, who ensures that he is able to follow the proceedings. The assumption is that, as a speaker of English-lexicon Creole, he should be able to follow the almost entirely English language proceedings of the Court.

Where particularly serious cracks are appearing in the system of justice, however, is in High Court proceedings involving trial by jury. Traditionally, property and related requirements restricted who could be selected for jury service. This favoured the more privileged sectors of the society, and ensured, therefore, that a significant proportion of those selected had a reasonable level of competence in English. As part of the decolonisation process, there has been a general tendency to liberalise the system of jury selection, and admit a much more representative cross-section of the population into jury service. This means, of course, that a larger number of persons with Creole as their dominant language and relatively little competence in English, now serve on juries. This has had contradictory effects on the rights of Creole speakers in these societies. It means, on one hand, that jurors are linguistically better able to handle evidence presented to the Court in Creole by Creole-speaking witnesses. However, on the other hand, jurors are now much less well equipped linguistically to deal with English, the official language of the Court. This is the language in which charges are read, and in which the jury is formally addressed by lawyers as well as the judge. The difficulty which monolingual Creole-speaking jurors have takes two forms. The first involves the problem of lay people confronted with specialised legal jargon. This would arise even in a monolingual speech community. The additional problem is, of course, their lack of competence in English, the official language of the Court.

In the post-independence Commonwealth Caribbean, many institutions which previously explicitly excluded the Creole-speaking mass of the population, have now been formally opened to them. However, offical language policies and practices within them have not been seriously altered. The result totally contradicts any pretence that the system has been democratised. Denying genuine participation on grounds of language can be a lot more subtle and much more difficult to combat than making such a denial explicitly on grounds of race or class. In these societies, language conscious-ness among the poor and the dispossessed is extremely low. Such persons are, therefore, likely to accept and justify their own exclusion by themselves pointing to the fact that they cannot speak 'proper', i.e. speak English.

The Mass Media

The Mass Media represents another area of official language use in
which English is accepted as the sole official medium of communication, but in which English has been subject to encroachments
from Creole. In the period since political independence, the Mass
Media, particularly the radio, has become more accessible to the
bulk of the population. As a result, the media have led to aim
messages at a much wider cross-section of the public than
previously. The language situation which emerged in the media as a
result of these changed circumstances is a rather complex one.

The Mass Media have conformed to official language policy,
treating English as the sole official language these societies. In the
media, therefore, English is, in theory at least, the variety which is
used as the written and Public-Formal language. The complex
situation comes about because, in the print medium such as the
newspaper, there is sometimes need to represent in writing the
informal language of the bulk of the population which is, of course,
Creole. And in the case of the broadcast media, particularly the
radio, there is sometimes need to use the informal variety, Creole,
in a medium which is essentialy Public-Formal.

In newspapers, English is the normal, unmarked language
variety used. However, there is very often need to deviate from this
norm. For example, cartoons, satirical and gossip columns, as well
as direct quotes from persons interviewed, often appear in some
form of Creole. In the case of cartoons, these involve representations of situations in which the spoken language is used. For such
representations to be realistic and effective for the largely Creole-
speaking audience, the normal spoken informal language of the
community, Creole, has to be employed. As for direct quotes from
individuals, it is sometimes necessary, for realism and effect, to
keep the utterance in its original Creole form. This is often
preferable to paraphrasing or translating the utterance into English. In the case of articles of a satirical and gossipy nature, these
are forms of writing aimed at imitating informal speech. The writers
of such articles, therefore, resort to the use of written Creole as a
stylistic device.

Let us now look at radio. The role of English as the only language
normally written can be seen in scripted programmes such as news
broadcasts, news commentaries, in documentaries, death annouce-
ments, etc. These are all broadcast in English. The use of English is
further reinforced by the fact that radio is a Public-Formal
medium, and English is the Public-Formal spoken language of the
usually well-educated persons, radio announcers included, who
appear most frequently on radio. As a result, formal interviews,
discussions of 'serious' topics, speeches, etc. broadcast on the
radio also tend to be in English. However, as in the case of the print

medium, Creole has managed to acquire an important though sub-ordinate role. One way in which this has come about is via the development of programmes which seek to provide the public with greater access to the radio. Such programmes include those of the public-opinion type, made up of either phone-calls from members of the public, or interviews recorded with the 'man-in-the-street'. The social origins of many of the contributors to such programmes are quite diverse. Many of these contributors, not having a command of English use their native language, Creole, instead. Radio, like the newspapers often employs Creole for purposes of realism and social authenticity. Thus, for example, radio drama and advertisements aimed at a mass audience, tend to include charac-ters who, in order to appear credible and true to life, have to speak Creole.

As with the education system and the legal system, Creole speakers have acquired, in the post-colonial era, greater access to the Mass Media. However, the degree to which the language of the media has adjusted to the language competence of its new audience, has been relatively minor. The normal unmarked lang-uage variety for writing and Public-Formal use within the media remains English. This would suggest that language is constituting a barrier to the Mass Media communicating as efficiently as it should with the Creole speaking mass of the population.

This, indeed, is one of the findings of Smalling (1983). She ran an intelligibility test on four news items broadcast by a Jamaican radio station. Two of the items dealt with Jamaican topics, one dealt with a topic of Caribbean interest, and the other was an international news item. These news items were taped and played to two groups. The first was a group of 10 Jamaican students of the Caribbean Institute of Mass Communications (CARIMAC) of the University of the West Indies in Jamaica. This group was to serve as the control group since, because of their high level of education, they could be presumed to have a high level of competence in English. The other group of informants consisted of 30 beginning students in an adult literacy class run by the JAMAL foundation. This group, because of their lack of formal education, could be considered representative of the monolingual Creole speaking section of the Jamaican population. Each news item was played for the infor-mants and a set of questions asked immediately before going on to the next item. The questions tested understanding of the news items in the areas of lexico-semantics and syntax. Interestingly, the university student group had scores which ranged from 56.25% to 93.15%, with an average (mean) score of 70%. It is interesting that the gap between the average (mean) score for this group and the highest score attained is, in fact, as large as 23.15%. This shows a surprisingly low level of intelligibility among even this group. The other group, the JAMAL students, scored an average (mean) of

50.2%, which meant that they scored 43.55% less than the highest score achieved in the text of 93.15%. (Smalling, 1983, pp. 46-49)

If we take the results of this admittedly very limited study and assume that the results could be generalised to the Creole speaking population of Jamaica as a whole, one gets some interesting results. With 43.55% as base figure, Smalling (1983, pp. 47-48) points out that, of the 115 minutes of news broadcast by R.J.R. (the radio station whose news items she used), 50.8 minutes could be regarded as wasted communication. She calculates that, in a 365 day year, the loss would amount to 699.6 hours. Calculated as a percentage of what it cost R.J.R. in 1983 to produce news broadcasts, this would represent a wastage of J$217,750. This, of course, is the wastage which occurs on only one section of the Mass Media. There is, as well, another radio station in Jamaica, in addition to television and the newspapers. What Smalling does not deal with is the nervous energy, time and effort, not to mention money, which is often wasted by members of the public as a result of misunderstanding information which is broadcast. For example, in one of the news items which Smalling tested, there was a report that the assets of the National Housing Trust had increased. Many of her informants misinterpreted this to mean that there had been an increase in the contributions which employed persons have to make to the Trust. Smalling (1983, p. 49) quite correctly raises the question of whether a country such as Jamaica could afford to waste its communication resources in this fashion.

Devonish (1978, 1980) had referred to the important role which the radio could play in promoting the Public-Formal use of Creole in the Caribbean, as well as in the process of Creole language standardisation. This had been the case with for example the French-lexicon Creoles of St. Lucia and Dominica. At last, however, the English-lexicon Creoles have also made their breakthrough.. Radio Central, one of three regional broadcasting units recently set up by the Jamaica Broadcasting Corporation, came on the air in late 1982. It broadcast its newscast about local happenings in Central Jamaica using Jamaican Creole. For those sectors of the society who identified with the linguistic status quo, this came as a shock. One such individual expressed himself in this way. 'I couldn't believe what I was hearing: what sounded like news over JBC Radio Central here being delivered in patois!' (Keating, 1982, p. 3) The reaction among certain circles was one not only of shock but of fear. It was as if something very close and dear to them was being threatened.

What are the facts surrounding this issue? Radio Central is a rural based radio station set up as an experiment in development support communication. It is aimed mainly at residents of farming communities in Central Jamaica. Before the station began broadcasting, U.S.A.I.D. sponsored a survey carried out through the

Ministry of Agriculture. Farmers in Central Jamaica were surveyed concerning their attitude to conventional news broadcasts put out in English by the established radio stations. They claimed they could not understand the big words used, nor could they cope with the accents of the announcers or their speed of delivery. This is a typical non-specialist view of what constitutes the major differences between Creole and English. The survey presented the farmers interviewed with three possible alternative ways in which the new regional station could broadcast its local newscast. The preferred format was one in which the main body of the news was presented in Creole. The news took the form of a casual conversation between two friends who share the latest news with each other and, as a result, with the listeners also. English was used only in the introduction to the news and in its conclusion, as well as in the inserts into the news of items such as interviews or recorded reports from news reporters. It is in this form that the local news on Radio Central has been broadcast as part of its daily three hour transmissions. (Bowen, 1982; Smalling, 1983, p. 50)

The fact that Creole speakers preferred to have their news transmitted to them in Creole in a Public-Formal medium such as the radio, contradicts a conventional view held by non-linguists and linguists alike. According to this view, Creole speakers have such a low linguistic self-image that they would reject any attempt to use Creole in official Public-Formal functions. The question is whether anyone has ever systematically asked Creole speakers for their opinions. More specifically, have Creole speakers been presented with concrete and viable alternatives which they could use as a basis for deciding on their language preferences?

There is one puzzling thing about the Radio Central experience, however. Radio Central is a regional unit of the government owned Jamaica Broadcasting Corporation (JBC). At the time when Radio Central came on the air, the attitude of the J.B.C. to language use on broadcasts originating from the capital could hardly be described as liberal. Around the same time, the Deputy Prime Minister of Jamaica, Hugh Shearer, publicly condemned the use of Creole on more than one occasion. There was, during the same period, a series of articles in the press, many written by prominent citizens, on the language question. Several of these articles were hostile to the use of Creole. One must add to this the hostile reception given to Radio Central's Creole newscasts among sections of the more privileged classes in Central Jamaica. Those who held political power in the society, as well as direct or indirect control of Radio Central, were extremely anti-Creole. It is, therefore, quite surprising that the newscast in Creole on Radio Central continued to be broadcast up until late 1984. It was only then presumably bowing to pressure, that Radio Central it is reported, stopped the programme.

To explain the longevity of this programme on Radio Central one may have to look at the source of funding for the radio station. The United States Agency for International Development (USAID) provided funds for the setting up of a series of regional radio stations in Jamaica of which Radio Central was one. In making the money available, USAID would have had as its main focus the provision of efficient means of communication with the rural population of Jamaica and their further integration into the existing socio-economic system. If Jamaican Creole happened to be the most efficient means of promoting this goal, then so be it. The very role of Radio Central as a USAID funded project allowed it the kind of autonomy not possible in any other section of the government-owned mass media. As a result, Radio Central was able to resist pressures from very powerful sections of the Jamaican ruling classes for nearly two years.. The approach of USAID in this case must have been very similar to the position which it took in Haiti in 1979. There, it had funded activities leading up to the introduction of Haitian Creole into the primary schools as the official medium of instruction. In Jamaica, as in Haiti, representatives of foreign capital provided funds to projects involving the expansion in functions of Creole, in total defiance of the views of important sections of the local political elite. The issue which was at stake for USAID was not that of the continued use of English as the medium for broadcasting news, or even the continued use of English as the sole official language in Jamaica. Rather, the issue was one of the survival and promotion of the socio-economic system existing in Jamaica.

We need, however, to also look at the reasons for the eventual demise of Radio Central news broadcasts in Creole. Pressure from certain privileged sections of the population can only provide a partial explanation since, for reasons already discussed, the radio station did have an unusual amount of room for manoeuvre. It is my view that the explanation lies in the limited vision which those in charge of the broadcasts had of what they were doing. Probably for the first time in the Jamaican mass media, as a result of a conscious decision, Jamaican Creole was being used as a medium for straightforward communication of information, minus any over-tones of humour, mimicry or folklore. For the broadcasters, they were simply broadcasting the 'Local news in the local language', as the programme was billed. They shared the idea widespread in Jamaican society that Jamaican Creole was a 'dialect' of English, a version of English which was pronounced differently. This resulted in the appearance in the broadcasts of huge chunks of speech which were English in both vocabulary and syntax. The following are just a few examples from the Radio Central news broadcast of 1st July, 1983.

> 1) *Di miiting waz chiered bai . . .*   'The meeting was chaired by . . .'
> 2) *. . . manita dem wata kansamshan . . .*   '. . . monitor their water consumption . . .'
> 3) *. . . how dem kyan put siefti fiicha in dem bildingz.*   '. . . how they can put safety features in their buildings.'
> 4) *Wat iz rieli kwait gud about it woz . . .*   'What was really quite good about it was . . .'
> 5) *Him se dat di kwaliti af werk waz af a veri hai standard.*   'He said that the quality of work was of a very high standard.'

Example 1 illustrates the use of English syntax in what is supposed to be a Creole utterance. It involves the use of the English passive form, a structure which does not exist in Creole. Examples 2 and 3 employ English vocabulary items such as 'monitor', 'consumption' and 'saftey feature' unchanged in the Creole news except for slight phonological modification. No effort was made to find or generate Creole equivalents for these terms. Examples 4 and 5 are particularly striking, involving as they do the extensive use of both English vocabulary **and** syntax. Vocabulary items not normally used in Creole, e.g. 'quality', 'standard', are employed. Syntactic structures borrowed from English such as the use of **iz** in Example 4 in a context where Creole would require no marker, should be noted. In addition, there is the choice of English lexical items such as 'quite' (Example 4) and 'very' (Example 5) to operate as intensifiers where Creole would employ devices such as reduplication (i.e. the repetition of the item which is to be intensified).

The language forms employed in the Radio Central newscasts opened the radio station to the criticism that it was not even using real Creole but a bastardised form of English. Ironically, this was an accusation made by one of those persons totally opposed to the principle of radio broadcasts in Creole. There was the additional problem of the extent to which such language use was allowing for effective communication with the mass of monolingual Creole speakers.. The use of a language variety with such a heavy influence from English was bound to erect again the very linguistic barriers which the use of Creole was intended to break down. These were all weaknesses which, no doubt, contributed to the demise of the Creole language broadcasts. However, these weaknesses were an expression of a more profound problem. This was the failure on the part of the Radio Central broadcasters to recognise Creole as a distinct and autonomous linguistic system, a language in its own right. As a result, no effort was made to promote language consciousness and language pride among the Creole-speaking communities receiving the broadcasts. In fact, the great deal of

English influence in the language used in the broadcasts may have
encouraged many listeners to have negative attitudes to their own
conservative rural Creole speech. In addition, no effort was made to
involve Creole speakers in the expansion in the functions of their
language by (i) encouraging critical public discussion around the
appropriateness and effectiveness of the language forms actually
used in the programme, and (ii) involving listeners in a process of
helping to develop suitable Creole translations for the range of
specialised terminology likely to occur in news broadcasts.

Against this background, when the Radio Central broadcasts
came under attack from those with a vested interesting in maintaining the linguistic status quo, there was no mass reaction in
support of the programme from those at whom it was directed. The
reason for this is obvious. Monolingual Creole speakers are
unlikely to have even been aware of the debate, taking place as it
did in English, usually in the form of newspaper articles and letters
to the editor. Such persons could only have known about the debate
and become involved in it if Radio Central itself had informed its
listeners about the discussion and provided them with a forum for
airing their views. As far as I can tell, this was not done to any
significant degree. Instead of being in a position to argue for the
extension of the use of Creole to other programmes which it
broadcast, Radio Central found itself having to argue in defence of
the small expansion in the functions of Creole already in place. The
station was on the defensive and without a support base among the
sections of the population at whom its Creole news broadcasts were
aimed. It was, therefore, just a matter of time, before the pressure
of the anti-Creole lobby became overwhelming.

As we have seen in this section, the post-colonial linguistic status
quo is beginning to crumble in the mass media. The most important
symbol of this crumbling has been the use of Creole as the main
language in its local news broadcasts. The fact that these broadcasts were eventually taken off the air is clearly only a temporary
setback. The effectiveness of Creole as a medium for communicating with the mass of the population is slowly over-riding the
symbolic value of English as the sole officially sanctioned language
in the mass media.

The Political System

Alleyne (1964) is one of the few analysts, and possibly the first, to
raise the question of the role of language in the political process of
the Commonwealth Caribbean. He was writing very early in the
post independence period of both Jamaica and Trinidad and
Tobago. His concern was with the language gap which existed
between the sections of the political elite who had inherited power,
and the Creole-speaking mass of the population on whose behalf
power was supposedly being exercised. With reference to Jamaica,

he states, 'And it is significant that in this period too, when the masses at last are given real constitutional rights in the form of the franchise, the linguistic situation contributes to the fact that spokesmen for the negro masses do not arise from the ranks of the masses but are drawn form other classes.' (Alleyne, 1964, p. 3) Alleyne then goes on to discuss some of the communication problems faced by the political elite at the time of independence in Jamaica. He discusses the difficulty faced by this group in conveying to the Creole-speaking mass of the population the significance of terms such as 'independence', 'freedom' and 'democracy', as well as the tremendous misinterpretations which took place.

Many non-linguists have dealt with the problem of communication within the political systems of these countries. However, because they accept the ruling class view that these societies are English speaking, they look at areas other than language for an explanation of the problem. For example, Stone (1980, pp. 61-62) attributes the communication problem within the Jamaican political system to the high level of illiteracy and functional illiteracy within the society. As an illustration of this hypothesis, he refers to a mass meeting of sugar estate workers which he attended. The meeting dealt with a local controversy over the lease of the estate farm to the workers. Eight speakers addressed the audience for three hours. A check by Stone at the end of the meeting suggested that 30 members of the audience he spoke to, only 5 had understood what the major issues of the controversy were about. (Stone, 1980, p. 69n) It is pretty obvious from the example cited by Stone, that the communication problem did not involve literacy as such, i.e. lack of ability to read on the part of the workers. Rather, the workers had problems understanding what was **said** to them by the eight speakers. This was a problem of understanding spoken English.

As will be established in the discussion on the education system, lack of competence in English is at the core of the illiteracy problem in these countries. Thus, this lack of competence occurs side by side with illiteracy. However, it is not illiteracy which causes inability to understand English or communicate effectively in it. Rather, it is the low competence in English which restricts the ability to exercise literacy skills in that language. Therefore, when dealing with the problem of communication within the political system, it is the language question which should be the focus of attention.

After independence, English continued as the official language of the political institutions within the state. Thus, English remained the language of Parliament and, as well, the language of government administration. In a more general sense, English remained the language of formal political life in these countries.

However, some modification in the area of language use did take place. With the existence of universal adult suffrage, politicians have found it necessary to court the Creole speaking populations via the use of **some** Creole in political speeches. Let us analyse what function this use of Creole actually performs in such speeches. Creole is used for sloganeering, telling jokes, abuse, and as an emotional rhetorical device. However, to the extent that many political speeches can be said to have any content, this content is expressed in English. The major issues of the day, be they to do with the Budget or foreign policy, are presented to the public and discussed by the political elite in English. Those people in the society with limited competence in English, therefore find it impossible to locate any publicly accessible source which could communicate with them about the major political issues of the day, in the language which they use and understand best.

All the governments of the Commonwealth Caribbean are publicly committed to the principle of periodic free and fair elections. However important such elections may be to the practice of democracy, the practice of democracy cannot be restricted to three minutes in a polling box every five years. Democracy as it is presently practised in these countries blocks, on grounds of language, the access of the mass of Creole speakers to information about political issues and decisions which affect their lives. This kind of democracy must be a farce. What is even more important is the right of Creole speakers to actively participate in public discussion. This is the only means available to them to actively influence the making of public policy, rather than remaining the passive recipients of such policy decisions.

The mass media is the forum which could potentially promote such participation. However, traditionally, these media have been organised to talk **at** the public. Nevertheless, there are some phone-in and man-in-the-street type programmes broadcast on the radio. These programmes are, in addition to all the non-linguistic criticisms which may be levelled at them, linguistically restrictive. Because of the social values associated with the medium of radio, a member of the public speaking on one of these programmes will usually only use Creole if and when he feels himself unable to use English. Moderators of such programmes may even resort to the use of Creole for purpose of effective communication. However, there is a shared value among all those involved that English is the language which ought to be used in such situations, when and where possible. Any use made of Creole occurs in circumstances where the speaker has made a conscious decision to violate this shared language value. Of course, monolingual Creole speakers, the majority of whom may lack the linguistic self-confidence to violate social expectations, will tend to opt to remain silent. As for letters to the editor in the newspapers, these are obviously linguistically even more restrictive.

The evidence suggests that the political elite in these countries is not entirely unaware of the linguistic problems which exist in their communication with the public. It seems likely that they are aware of the communication gap and manipulate it to their own advantage. Thus, the political institutions of the state can be made to go through the **forms** of public consultation, with public statements, policy declarations, etc., without any of these being challenged by public opinion. However, when the same political elite does, for some unusual reason, genuinely want to communicate with the mass of the population, it resorts to the use of Creole.

A recent situation in Guyana serves to illustrate the above observation. A speaker's guide was prepared to government ministers who were supposed to take part in public 'fan-out' exercise in March, 1982. The object of the exercise was to explain to the Guyana population that the country was then bankrupt. One of the instructions in the guide was 'use creolese - but don't overdo it'. *(Catholic Standard* March 28, 1982, p. 1) The same population which had not been consulted, and most certainly not in Creolese, i.e. Guyanese Creole, over the economic and political decisions which led to the bankruptcy, were being informed in Creolese of the terrible effects of these decisions. The 'don't overdo it' bit is important. The writers of the guide are aware that, insofar as any consultation with the Creole speaking public has ever taken place, this was done in English. Any attempt by government ministers, therefore, to lay the Creole line on too thickly would, of course, cause suspicion among the population about the motive for so drastic a change in language behaviour. In the post colonial period, English was retained as the language of official political life. Nevertheless, as a result of the increased political importance of Creole-speakers, use of Creole has crept into certain important areas within the political system. However, in cases such as these, Creole plays a purely subordinate and subsidiary role to English, the official language.

The Education System

The education system is perhaps the only area in which an **explicit** official language policy has emerged in the post-independence period. An important reason for this is the central role which the School plays in these societies. The School is expected to reproduce and reinforce norms of language use and language acceptability, particularly in official and public-formal domains. Most recent discussion on language education policy within the Commonwealth Caribbean has tended to assume that the education system **creates** the socio-economic and linguistic order in the society. In reality, the education system is intended to reproduce the prevailing socio-economic and linguistic order by doing two things. Firstly, it aims to induce an ideological acceptance by the mass of the population of the status quo, linguistic and socio-economic. Secondly, and in the course of trying to achieve the first objective, it aims at providing skills required by the labour force. These skills are needed by workers in order to produce for those who own and control the means of production. Thus, official language education policy is not created by the education system or within it.This policy is, in the first instance, determined by the state, and ultimately by those who own and control the means of production.

The education system inherited from the colonial power was one in which English, in addition to being a subject to be taught, was the sole medium by which literacy was acquired as well as the sole medium of instruction. The assumption underlying this language education policy was that those who entered the education system were, in fact, native-speakers of English, English-lexicon Creole being no more than a form of 'broken English' which had to be corrected by the education system. As part of the realisation of nationalist aspirations immediately before and after independence, the education system was rapidly expanded to include large numbers of the Creole-speaking mass of the population who had, as a group, been previously excluded. The new linguistic reality of the post-independence era was of an education system involving a vast majority of Creole-speakers with very limited competence in English. The official myth that competence in English could be created by either ignoring Creole or correcting it, was severely put to the test. And it failed the test. Very soon, members of the ruling classes and their spokesmen could be heard complaining that the skills in reading, writing and speaking English among the products of the expanded education system were extremely limited.

It was at this point during the late 1960's and early 1970's, that academic expertise, notably that of linguists involved in the study of Caribbean Creole languages, was drafted in to help find solutions to the language related education problems then and still affecting these societies. Here is how Lawrence Carrington, one of the linguists concerned with the question, analyses the problem as it exists in Trinidad and Tobago. This analysis could however be applied to any of the countries of the Commonwealth Caribbean. According to Carrington (1978a, p. 15), traditionally there was a great deal of correspondence between the pupils, the teachers and the educational goals, at the level of language. Pupils would have had relatively adequate exposure to English. The teachers would have had reasonable competence in English. And as for language education policy, the aim was to teach English, use it as a medium for teaching literacy and, as well, use it as the sole medium of instruction. With the democratisation of the education system, and the admission of large numbers of both teachers and pupils from Creole speaking backgrounds, in Carrington's view, a crisis developed. He describes the crisis as follows. '. . . the pupils, the teachers, methods and goals matched each other (in times past) to a degree that is not present in contemporary Trinidad and Tobago. At the present time, teachers and pupils match each other more closely than either of them matches the goals and teaching methods of the education system'. (Carrington, 1978a, p. 15) Such a situation poses severe problems for an education system which continues, in the post colonial period, to use English as the sole medium for teaching literacy and the sole official medium of instruction.

The ideological framework within which linguistic expertise approached the problem was that of total acceptance of ruling class authority. Thus, Craig (1980, p. 15) states, 'In the final analysis, it is not the prerogative of the Language Educator to stipulate what language policy should or should not be followed: that is the prerogative of the state or some competent authority within the state'. So, according to this view, if the state or some competent authority within the state proposes language policies which result in the denial of language rights to a large section of the population, the duty of the linguist or Language Educator is to implement such policies and make them work!

Lawrence Carrington provides in his work a classic example of the ideological blinkers with which Caribbean linguists approached the language in education issue. It is, of course, obvious that one cannot discuss questions of language education policy without dealing with the general official language policy of the society. In fact, it is the general official language policy of the society which provides the overall direction for language education policy. Carrington (1976) provides a long and detailed discussion of whether English or Creole should be the medium of instruction in the education systems of the Commonwealth Caribbean. Interestingly, in the course of the entire discussion, he makes no provision for the possibility that Creole could become an/the official language of any of the countries concerned. Carrington, in a later work, actually states, 'We are not at the start of a process and making a decision about what language ought to be official in a mythical new society'. (sic) (Carrington, 1978a, p. 16) Ignoring the possibility of Creole becoming an/the official language of these societies, his conclusions would quite naturally be biased in favour of the retention of English as the official medium of instruction.

In spite of the criticisms expressed here, the work of Caribbean linguists has had a positive effect on the language education policies of many of these countries. There is widening recognition within official circles that Creole speaking children do come into the education system speaking a language variety possessing rules and structure. It is also becoming accepted that the native language of such children should be respected within the school, and that English should be taught as an additional language rather than as a replacement for their native language. It should be stressed here, however, that for both linguists and education authorities, this recognition of Creole is seen purely as a means of facilitating the acquisition of English. A knowledge of the pupil's language background makes it easier to design materials and methods for effectively teaching him English. Also, a pupil who is not made to feel linguistically insecure because of his Creole language background, is more likely to acquire an effective command of English. Limited as this enlightenment is, it has only taken place in the Ministries of Education of Jamaica, Trinidad and Tobago, and Guyana, and according to Carrington (1978b, pp. 86-87), still remains to be spread to the education authorities of the other countries. In spite of this, however, it is evident that official language education policy has slowly and reluctantly started to shift. The pressure for this has come from the sheer numbers of predominantly Creole speakers which the post-colonial education systems have to deal with.

New teaching materials have had to be designed to support this new and more liberal attitude to the issue of language in education. One such set of materials is the course called *The Primary Language Arts* designed for Jamaican schools. It is a course which attempts to teach literacy skills in English to children who come from Creole language backgrounds. One of the authors has this to say about the only section of the course which requires the use of **spoken** English by pupils. '... the Controlled Talk exercises. .. are not intended as a course in **spoken Standard English.** The main intention is that they should make the form and meaning of new structures familiar to the child before he comes upon them in his reading.' (Wilson, 1977, p. 176) (my emphasis) Thus, teaching spoken English as such, is not a major goal. But this course is being implemented in a society where English is, at least in theory, the official spoken medium of Parliament, the Law Courts, the electronic mass media, etc.! Therefore, regardless of the literacy skills the Creole speaking child may acquire in English, he/she may still find it difficult to **actively** and creatively participate in any domain where spoken English is required. Whether the developers of this set of teaching materials realise it or not, they are helping to reproduce the prevailing socio-economic order within the society. They are attempting to produce members of the labour force who would have skills in reading and writing English, and even the ability to understand spoken English. A literate work force is much more productive than one which is illiterate. In addition, foreign investors, largely from English-speaking North America, do not even have to go to the trouble and expense of translating written instructions, etc. into the language of the local work force. These are all benefits to be enjoyed by employers of labour. As for the members of the labour force themselves, the fact that the *Primary Language Arts* course does not train them in the use of spoken English, has negative implications. Creole-speakers may be denied the opportunity to participate actively and effectively in official and public-formal domains where English is the expected medium of communication.

There is another elitist aspect of *The Primary Language Arts* course. In fact, this aspect is one which exists in all approaches which use English as the medium for teaching literacy to Creole speakers. Craig argues that the urgent need for literacy in these societies can be more easily satisfied by the use of English rather than the use of written Creole. He attempts to justify his position by arguing that '. . . where vocabulary is largely held in common, differences such as those between English and Creole or the mesolect present no barriers to the acquisition of reading and writing in English **at elementary levels.** It is rather at the more advanced levels of reading, where grammatical cues which go beyond mere vocabulary become important, that differences of the relevant kind cause serious problems.' (Craig, 1980, p. 13) (my emphasis) For those who support this kind of position, therefore, reading and writing at 'elementary levels' is all that the Creole-speaking mass of the population need. The 'more advanced levels' of reading and writing are, no doubt, going to be the preserve of those groups or classes in the society who are adequately exposed to English. In essence, therefore, this kind of approach to literacy teaching is intended to establish a two-tiered system of literacy acquisition. People with a mainly Creole language background will attain 'elementary levels' of literacy, whereas those who have adequate exposure to English will attain 'more advanced levels'. What is significant is that this is not an unforeseen occurrence. However, for those who support this kind of approach, such an outcome is preferable to using Creole as a medium for teaching literacy.

This unsatisfactory state of affairs at the level of the formal education system, expresses itself at the level of adult ability to employ literacy skills learnt via English. In Jamaica, the adult literacy organisation, JAMAL, carried out a Communications Skills Survey. A representative sample of the population over the age of 15 years was surveyed. They were asked two simple questions in writing which they were expected to respond to also in writing. 21.8% of the sample were totally illiterate, could not read nor write. 18.8% could 'read and write well'. What is of particular

interest, was the group that showed impaired literacy skills. 2.1% of
the sample could write 'but not make sense'. Another 8.1% could
write 'but make very little sense'. And 28.3% could write 'with
incorrect grammar'. (JAMAL Communications Skills Survey, cited
in Carrington, 1980, pp. 148-149)

In commenting on the group that could write 'with incorrect
grammar',Carrington (1980, pp. 148-149) points out that given
contemporary non-specialist views of language in Jamaica, this
group probably included (i) those who made grammatical errors
resulting from lack of competence in English, and (ii) those who
produced grammatically correct Jamaican Creole structures de-
eemed by the assessors of the test responses as incorrect grammar.
I would suggest that Carrington's point is even more true of the
groups who wrote but who made either 'no sense' or 'very little
sense'. This would mean that 38.5% of the sample suffered, to
varying degrees, from limitations imposed on their literacy. This
was caused by the fact that they had a limited degree of competence in the language in which they were using their literacy
skills. The group who suffered from this limitation constituted 67%
of those in the sample who were able to write at all. If one
generalises the results of this survey to the Jamaican population as
a whole, what is particularly significant is not simply the high rate of
illiteracy. It is the large number of the literate population who, at
great expense to the society, have acquired literacy, only to have
that literacy restricted by the lack of competence in English, the
language in which literacy was taught. Every indication suggests
that the plight of Creole-speaking literates in the other English-
lexicon Creole speech communities of the Commonwealth Caribbean is no better than in Jamaica.

Can these countries afford this kind of wastage of human and
material resources? The answer, of course, is no. However, the
post-colonial ruling class is faced with a dilemma. As in other
Caribbean Creole speech communities such as Haiti, the demand
for a functionally literate work force is fast outstripping the ability
of the society to provide such literacy via the official European
language. If, however, the ruling class were to bow to pressure and
the logic of the situation, and sanction the use of Creole as an
official medium for teaching literacy, they would have lost an
important expression of their class dominance. This involves the
special role which they play as a group having privileged access to
the only written and official language in the society. Not, of course,
that the ruling class could not ideologically readjust, if they had to,
to a modified linguistic status quo. They have done so, with
remarkable ease, in Haiti. Nevertheless, the rulers within countries
of the Commonwealth Caribbean will only institute language
reforms if they have to, particularly if pressure is exerted, as was
the case in Haiti, by important external financial interests. As it is,

the cracks are only now becoming obvious in the policies on language in education.

These cracks have been big enough to force a reconsideration of position by some of the technical experts involved in the issue. During the 1970's, Carrington had been the proponent of a position which presumed the continued use of English as the sole medium of instruction in these countries. In a change of position, however, Carrington (1980, p. 187) shifted to a view which favours the teaching of literacy in the native language of the learners. He feels that English, as well as literacy in English, must be taught. It should however, be treated as an exercise in teaching a new language to an already literate individual.

The Caribbean Lexicography Project

While the language rights of the Creole-speaking population across the Commonwealth Caribbean continue to be violated, the English-speaking elite have not been slow to set about tackling their own language problems. The Caribbean Lexicography Project set up by Richard Allsopp and based in Barbados, should, in my view, be considered as an effort to tackle one such problem. The project is concerned with codifying the lexicon (vocabulary) of the variety of English spoken by educated Caribbean speakers of English. The Dictionary of Caribbean English Usage which will be produced by the project will '. . . be concerned more particularly with the English usage at the middle and upper level of the educational (not the social) scale, while paying due attention to the underlying influence of dialect at all levels and throughout the region.' (Allsopp, 1972, p. 5) (emphasis in the original)

The quotation above is extremely interesting. The reason for this is the emphasis which he places on the fact that the project is concerned with the English usage of the middle and upper levels of the educational scale, not the social scale. One immediately wonders why, since the two scales overlap considerably, is Allsopp so emphatic about the distinction? The fact is, of course, that the class which inherited the state machinery from the colonialists came from the educated sectors of the Caribbean population, i.e. the middle class or petty bourgeoisie. It is these people who, in Allsopp's terms, make up the 'middle and upper levels of the educational scale'. The reason for Allsopp not wishing to refer to the social scale is clear. The section of the middle class who now constitute the political elite could hardly, if one takes into account their economic base or their social background, be considered to occupy the upper levels of the social scale, i.e. to be members of the upper class.

Initially, the indigenous political elite defined its own distinct national identity in relation to the bourgeoisie of the ex-colonial power, Britain. In time, as U.S. and Canadian economic interests became dominant, the definition of national identity started to be made more and more in relation to the bourgeoisies of these countries. It is significant that Britain, U.S. and Canada are all officially English speaking countries. Thus, the nationalism of the Commonwealth Caribbean English speaking political elite needed to be expressed at the level of language, without eroding their special privileges as speakers of English in their own societies. The Caribbean Lexicography Project and the dictionary which it will produce serves this purpose perfectly. It defines a Standard Caribbean English, distinct in various ways from Standard British, American or Canadian English, and even more distinct from trhe Creole language varieties spoken in the various Commonwealth Caribbean countries.

The above interpretation of the class nature of the project can be seen in the following justification which Allsopp presents. He states that colonialism had two effects, '. . . it imposed **British** English as the desirable standard in all matters of Anglophone Caribbean language (not just syntax but actually pronunciation and vocabulary); it also instilled a sense of apology in all Caribbean speakers of English for every aspect of their local English that differentiated it from British English. The local English in question was, of course, not the "dialect", which the apologetic look upon as a shameful relic, but "real" English - literate English.' (Allsopp, 1972, p. 2) (emphasis in the original) He adds that this kind of approach still conditions 'educated' attitudes today. The Caribbean Lexicography Project is aimed, among other things, at combatting these negative attitudes to their own variety of English among the Caribbean educated elite. In order to achieve this, the project will compile a Dictionary of Caribbean English Usage, based on the English of those who belong to the middle or upper end of the educational scale in the Caribbean. This project does **not** address itself to the language problems faced by the Creole speaking populations of the region, nor is it intended to. More than this, Allsopp (1978, p. 182), in the process of demonstrating the usefulness of the project, explicitly denies the possibility of any English lexicon-Creole in the Commonwealth Caribbean ever becoming an official language in its own right.

An Analysis Within a Theoretical Framework

This is an attempt to continue the theorectical discussion first raised in the final section of Chapter 1, in the light of the information about the Caribbean language situation already presented. In the Caribbean countries already discussed, one can say that the economic system is one of capitalism. However, the economies of these societies are not of the industrial capitalist type. Rather, they are generally based either on the export of raw materials and/or on tourism. However, the trend is in the direction of some degree of industrialisation. Ideological state apparatuses are simultaneously required to both include and exclude the mass of the population who make up the labour force. An apparatus such as the education system is, on one hand, required to reproduce the skills of the labour force and to promote an ideological acceptance of the socio-economic system. It simultaneously is required to exclude the bulk of the population from access to higher education, and hence from access to participation in the decision-making processes in the society. This analysis is equally applicable to any other ideological state apparatus. For example, the political system both includes the mass of the population in very often allowing them a vote. It, however, prevents them from being able to actively involved in the formation of government policy.

In advanced industrial capitalist societies, there is definite shift in the direction of increased emphasis on the integrating aspects of these apparatuses. Because, however, there continues to be private ownership of the means of production, complete integration of the non-owning classes into these apparatuses cannot take place. With the Creole-speaking Caribbean moving in the direction of some form of industrial development, one would expect a greater emphasis being placed on the integrative functions of these apparatuses than hitherto. At the level of language, the traditional emphasis on exclusion would have created a situation of quite rigid diglossia. With the shift in emphasis in the contemporary situation, diglossia could be expected to partly break down, but not to disappear.

Another factor which needs to be taken into account is the state of national and class consciousness within the mass of the population. This consciousness often results in political pressure leading to greater access to these apparatuses, e.g. the education system. On the other hand, the liberalisation induced by a shift in the direction of industrialisation, also serves to stimulate national and class consciousness. In many situations in the Caribbean, language consciousness goes hand in hand with the other forms of consciousness.

In Guadeloupe, for example changes occured initially in the way that agricultural workers saw themselves. The rise in their trade union and political militancy was accompanied by an increase in Creole language consciousness. This language awareness eventually found formal expression in the policies of the agricultural workers' union (U.T.A.) and, more generally, the independence movement. The recognition by the central government of France that Creole should be treated as a regional language was consistent with its own language policies within the metropole. However, this

limited concession by the colonising power came only in response
to popular pressure in Guadeloupe, supported by nationalist
moves to develop the resources of the language. To varying degrees
in Aruba, Bonaire and Curacao, and in Surinam, St. Lucia and
Dominica, changes in popular consciousness on the Creole language question started off the shift in official language policy. In
Haiti and in the Commonwealth Caribbean, popular ideas about
Creole have been changing. However, it has been the failure of the
ideological state apparatuses in these countries to perform their
integrative functions efficiently which led to modifications in
official language policies and practices. These modifications have
generally involved the use of Creole in new domains, e.g. the lower
levels of the education system, certain sections of the mass media,
etc. Regardless of the immediate source of the pressure for
modifications, the result is a change in the distribution of functions
of the two languages within the diglossia.

In all the Creole language situations discussed up to now in this
study, it is only the integrative functions of the state apparatuses
which have been thrown open to Creole. In the pre-20th century
period, it was religious education which was made available in
Creole in places like the Danish Virgin Islands, Aruba, Bonaire and
Curacao, and in Surinam. In modern times, the emphasis has shifted
to use of Creole in the lower levels of the education system. In
addition, advertisements and other messages in the media aimed at
the Creole-speaking population are frequently in Creole. This is
not to mention certain more superficial forms of political discourse,
as well as some forms of literature and poetry.

However, in what have traditionally been areas of exclusion for
the Creole-speaking population, very little has changed. The legal
system operates almost entirely in the official European language,
as does government administration. The higher levels of the
education system are still the preserve of the official European
language, as is the dissemination of the scientific and technical
information. According to the official view, Creole languages are
not capable of performing such functions because of the lack of
technical terminology, etc. The official position does not take the
view that such problems can and should be resolved in order to
open up the widest range of communication possibilities to Creole
speakers. Official diglossia has remained in place, even if the guise
is modified and the rhetoric softened. An exercise such as that in
which the Caribbean Lexicography Project is involved, is not
objectionable in itself. However, it is firmly based on the notion
that the existing diglossia can and should continue.

Diglossia in those areas of the state apparatuses which function
to exclude the mass of the population from participation, is very
difficult to combat unless Creole-speakers and organisations which
represent them have access to state power. In the light of the

analysis in this section, the following chapter will deal with proposals on the kind of official language policies which would help achieve the goal of national liberation in the Caribbean.

CHAPTER 6.

Language Reform In The Commonwealth Caribbean: Recommendations

In this chapter, we will examine the question language reform in those countries in the Commonwealth Caribbean where an English-lexicon Creole is widely spoken. Many of the issues raised would be of relevance to other Creole language situations in the region. However, in order to be able to make concrete and specific recommendations, it was necessary to narrow the focus of the discussion down to a group of speech communities which share a great deal in common with each other. In the discussion on language reform which follows, the major point of interest concerns what can and should be done on the language question by those who hold state power. Democratic official language policies and practices can be achieved in one of two ways. Political power may come into the hands of representatives of the Creole-speaking majority of the population, and appropriate measures are taken to deal with the language question. Otherwise, popular pressure may be brought to bear on those holding state power, forcing some degree of language reform.

Some General Principles

The major goal of official language policy reform in the Commonwealth Caribbean should be to provide access. All institutions, areas of knowledge, information and general culture should be available to every individual in the society, regardless of language background. The general way in which this is phrased is quite deliberate. Speakers of language varieties other than English-lexicon Creole also suffer deprivation of their language rights in the countries of their birth. The plight of minorities who speak American Indian languages in Guyana and Belize, including Garefuna (the language of the 'Black Caribs' of Belize), are particularly worthy of mention. There are, as well, East Indian speakers of Bjojpuri in Trinidad and Guyana, and French Creole speaking minorities in Trinidad and Grenada who ought not to be forgotten. Nevertheless, the focus will be on the roles and functions of English-lexicon Creoles, the majority language in all these countries with the exception of St. Lucia and Dominica.

The principle stated above is, of course, an ideal. The question that faces us is the steps that we need to take to move at least some distance in the direction of achieving that ideal. The practical requirement is that the official use of Creole be extended into as many domains as possible which were previously the exclusive preserve of English. The extension of the official use of Creole into every new domain represents the removal of the linguistic barrier blocking the Creole speaking mass of the population from participation in that domain. Some realism is necessary at this point, however. It is inevitable that English will remain an important supplementary language for the foreseeable future. The reason for this is the special role which English plays as a technical language in areas such as the drafting of legislation, higher administration, and advanced areas of science and technology. It is true that Creole, like any other language, can potentially carry out of these specialised functions. However, a considerable period of planning, preparation of specialised word-lists, etc. would be necessary before Creole could assume these functions. This is the kind of operation that goes on at a much more advanced stage of the language planning process than we are at right now. The correct focus, at present, has to be on extending the official use of Creole to areas of direct and immediate concern to the mass of the Creole speaking population.

The above concession to the continued role of English in certain specialised areas has implications for official language policy as a whole. The sensible position, in these circumstances, would be to give recognition to both English and Creole as official languages. However, it should not be lost sight of that the whole purpose of the language reform is to make Creole the major language of official internal communication in these countries.

The use of Creole as an official language should have the following objectives:

(a) It should encourage the participation of the ordinary monolingual speakers of Creole in the decision-making processes within their communities and within their nation as a whole.

(b) It should facilitate the exchange of new ideas, technologies, etc., a process which can only be achieved by means of a language variety which is as completely understood as is possible, and which the mass of the population can use in a totally creative manner.

(c) It should encourage the sort of literacy among the population which would involve the creative use of the skills of reading and writing, which could, in turn, contribute to people being able to better understand and change the communities in which they live.

There is a standard objection to the use of Creole as an official language in these countries. It is often argued that the prevailing language situation has '. . . the advantage to the community of possessing a national language which is at the same time international in its acceptability.' (Craig, 1978, p. 105) If, by 'the community' is meant the tiny English speaking elites who control these Caribbean societies, then the statement has validity. However, for the large mass of the primarily Creole speaking populations, the prevailing situation has no such advantage. In fact, the prevailing situation has two huge disadvantages for Creole speakers. It excludes them from access to both the official language of internal communication and the language of external communication. These functions are both performed by English. With Creole as an official language in these countries, Creole speakers would, at least, have access to a language of official internal communication. And, for the mass of the population and, in fact, for any member of the society, internal communication is of **primary** importance. This is true regardless of how important external communication may be to particular individuals, groups or the society at large. Creole as an official medium of communication therefore has the advantage of making accessible to the Creole speaking majority one of the two important networks of communication. And the one which is made accessible happens to be the more important of the two.

The Planning and Development of Caribbean English Lexicon Creoles

The Writing System:

The basis for a writing system for Caribbean English-lexicon Creoles already exists. The Cassidy Phonemic writing system which was developed for Jamaican Creole, has been used, with minor modifications for the representation of other English-lexicon Creoles in the Caribbean by linguists. No rival system exists. In addition, Cassidy (1978) proposed a modified version of his original phonemic writing system which could be used without modification for all the English lexicon Creoles of the area. What is, therefore, necessary at this stage is the relatively simple step of transforming what is basically a linguist's writing system into a set of writing conventions which could be taught to and be used by the Creole speaking populations at large.

Morpho-Syntax:

The area of morpho-syntax or what may be termed the grammatical structure, is of particular importance in discussing English-lexicon Creoles in the Commonwealth Caribbean. The reason is that this is one of the areas in which Creole differs most from English. In addition, because of a similarity between the vocabulary of Creole and English, there has been a tendency for them to develop a series of language varieties in between the most Creole varieties of language, on one hand, and the most standard varieties of English, on the other. This range of language varieties in between Creole, on one hand, and English, on the other, is what is referred to as the Creole continuum. Linguists have usually pointed to the existence of the continuum as a serious barrier to the use of Creole as an official language. The question normally asked is that of which variety along the continuum is going to be selected for use as the official language. The work of many Creole native speakers, notably Solomon (1972) and Gibson (1982) suggests that the varieties at the intermediate levels of the continuum share a common grammatical system with the more obviously Creole varieties. What differs is that the intermediate varieties tend to have surface forms which superficially resemble English much more than do forms used in the more Creole varieties. What then should be the approach to the question of the continuum? A democratic approach would be to avoid imposing a single variety of Creole on everyone in the society. Otherwise, the language planning process would be copying the very same intolerant language attitudes it is in the process of rejecting. The solution would be to (i) develop a description of the range of intermediate varieties of Creole along the continuum, all of which would be considered as acceptable forms of Creole, and (ii) identify certain forms which are most common and likely to widely known, which could be recommended for use by journalists, broadcasters, and others who find themselves in important positions as disseminators of information in Creole. This last recommendation is not intended as a means of necessarily creating a 'standard' variety of Creole. It is intended purely as a medium for identifying the most efficient variety of Creole for communicating with as wide a cross-section of the population as is possible. (See Devonish, 1978)

Vocabulary Elaboration:

There will be need for the systematic development of new Creole vocabulary items to deal with the communication requirements of the new functions which Creole would have to perform as an official language. This process will have to involve the generation of new vocabulary items which would be intelligible to Creole speakers. Borrowing from English therefore has to be restricted and the processes of word formation in Creole exploited to the full.

The Institutional Framwork:

Regardless of whether there is initial government support or not, it is possible to extend the range of official functions which Creole performs. Obviously, without government support, this task is much more difficult. It is, however, often the case that language promotion activities can serve to pressure governments into cooperating. In all this, it is absolutely necessary that Creole language promotion organisations be democratically constituted with adequate representation from among the Creole-speaking mass of the population. In addition, such organisations need to maintain an independence from direct political control. Mordecai (1979, p. 19) expresses great fear of language policy-making activity being subverted at the hands of rival political factions. The problems faced by the Creole language planning process in St. Lucia may not be an example of this, but it does indicate the vulnerability of language planning processes in conditions where there is political factionalism. (Carrington, 1981, pp. 8-9) The promotion of Creole is a deeply political task, involving as it does the promotion and defence of the language rights of the Creole speaking mass of the population. On the other hand, however, it is not a partisan political issue. Creole is the common possession of all, ironically, even those who despise it and attack it. It is important to stress that independence from direct political influence and control must be preserved, even in dealing with political parties and governments who are committed to the Creole cause.

The Implementation Of The Use of Creole In Official Domains

The Radio:

Although an important breakthrough for Creole, the use of Creole on Radio Central in Jamaica has been approached by the broadcasters involved with a certain amount of naiveté and, perhaps, a lack of understanding of the significance of what was being attempted. What follows is a linguist's view of how broadcasting in Creole could be introduced in a manner which would be designed to efficiently deal with the language problems which are likely to arise.

1) A team could be set up involving people with some linguistics background collaborating with a group of broadcasters. The initial focus of the team's work could be around the preparation for broadcast of a news and current affairs programme, mixed perhaps with popular Caribbean music, to be broadcast daily at peak listening time. One reason for selecting a news and current affairs type programme is that it would contain material of some importance to the lives of the Creole-speaking mass of the population. Yet, this kind of programme has always been broadcast in English. Another reason for selecting this programme type is that the broadcast of such a programme and its acceptance by the public, could constitute a significant psychological breakthrough for Creole. For the first time, many people would be forced to admit that Creole could perform a 'serious' function. The music would be used to avoid the staid format in which such programmes are often broadcast, and as a result, attract a greater Creole speaking audience.

2) In order to get such a programme off the ground, a great deal of preliminary work would be necessary. (a) The broadcasters would need to learn and use a Creole orthography based on the Cassidy writing system, (b) The particular morpho-syntatic forms which would be used in the Creole which is broadcast need to be identified and discussed, and (c) A preliminary word list of Creole equivalents for common English news and current affairs terms needsto be compiled. In the case of the word list, Creole speaking members of the target community ought to be consulted and asked to provide their own Creole translations for concepts which have been explained in them.

3) Based on the steps taken in '2', a set of preliminary programmes could be prepared and pre-tested. Having made the necessary modifications as a result of the reactions to the pre-test, the series of programmes could then be prepared and broadcast.

4) As the Public-Formal use of Creole becomes established among both broadcasters and listeners, interviews with public personalities could be introduced into the programmes. The persons interviewed could be explicitly asked to use Creole. This would serve to reinforce the image of Creole as a language of Public-Formal interaction.

5) The team in charge of the project would need to initiate some kind of formal training in translating from English into Creole for script-writers. This would be important at this point

because it is at this stage that foreign news may be phased into the programme. This would make it vital that people involved in producing the programme are able to provide effective translations from English into Creole.

6) With the expansion and development of Creole programming on the radio, it may be considered necessary to produce a news-sheet, a booklet, or a magazine in Creole to complement the Creole language programming. This printed material would be intended as a model for others who may wish to attempt to use written Creole themselves, e.g. the established newspapers, creative writers, etc., and who may wish to have a model which they could pattern themselves after. One of the functions of this publication would be to develop interesting and attractive ways of presenting the new Creole orthography which was developed initially for purposes of the programme. As well, the television and the established newspapers could be used as media for publicising this orthography.

As can be seen from the above, I conceive of the radio playing a central role in the process of making Creole an official and Public-Formal language.

Public Information:

It is positively dangerous to send out information connected with people's physical survival in a language which they may, at best, only partially understand. Thus, information about natural disasters such as hurricanes, floods, etc. must be communicated to the population via Creole. The same is true for information concerning threats to health, e.g. epidemics.

In the area of public information about the major political and economic issues of the day, Creole needs to be used as a language of public information. Since, for the immediate future, English is going to remain the language of most official public discussion on these matters, something needs to be done to protect the interests of the Creole speaking populations. It is possible for radio stations to broadcast synopses of deliberations of Parliament in Creole. These stations could also broadcast explanations in Creole of the major issues of national concern, e.g. balance of payments problems, the international recession, etc.

The proposals made in this section are very basic and do not require much effort or money to implement. Yet, from a practical point of view, they could significantly affect the lives of large numbers of Creole speakers in these countries.

The Law Courts:

There is need to train special officers of the Court whose duty it would be to provide translations from English into Creole or Creole into English on request from anyone involved in a case in court. This facility should also be made available to jurors. Many people, unfortunately, are going to feel much too embarrassed to publicly admit that they do not understand English and need the services of an interpreter. The courts and the systems of justice in these countries are going to have to carry out a serious programme of public education which would encourage people to view the use of an interpreter as a natural part of the exercise of their legal rights.

The Education System:

There are two views on the question of the role which the education system should play in relation to the implementation of official language policy. One view, seemingly one held by the Haitian education authorities, is that the education system is the place where new official language policy should first be implemented. This view argues that if you want to elevate the status and functions of a low prestige Caribbean Creole language, the place to do it is in the classroom. According to this line of reasoning, the very use of a language in the education process, as a medium for acquiring literacy, etc., establishes the validity of the language in the eyes of the pupils as well as the society at large. In my view, this kind of approach is a recipe for confusion, non-cooperation and resistance to language education measures by teachers and parents alike.

My position is that the language problems of the school are the language problems of the society at large. The denial of language rights of Creole speaking children within the classroom is of the same order as the denial of language rights which their parents are experiencing outside. It seems, therefore, that a reform in language education policy cannot take place outside of a more general reform in the roles and functions of the various languages used within the society as a whole. In circumstances where the language reform measures of the type suggested earlier are being imple-mented, the necessary measures within the education system would tend to follow quite naturally. In a situation where Creole is a major medium of public information, and a language used as a medium of written communication in pamphlets, newsheets, maga-zines, etc., the preconditions have already been created in which there is a need in the society for literacy in Creole. Any measure to introduce Creole as a medium for teaching initial literacy in schools is less likely to run into serious opposition in these circumstances.

It is, therefore, through the socio-political battles in the society outside that those who hold power may be made more responsive to the language rights of the Creole speaking mass of the population. It is, in turn, this responsiveness which creates conditions in the education system which allows to be applied the psycho-linguistic principle that '... children should be educated through the medium of their own languages..' (Carrington, 1982, p. 6) Carrington, in fact, put this forward as a basic starting point for the formulation of language education policy in the Caribbean.

Let us examine the extent to which the above principle is supported by research in the area of bilingual education. Cummins (1979, pp. 222-251), in an extensive analysis of research done in this area, reaches the following conclusions:

1)   In circumstances where a bilingual child's first language was dominant or at least prestigious, his exposure to a second language via the school system poses no threat to his first language. He simply acquires an additional language variety as part of his linguistic repertoire, a process referred to as additive bilingualism. On the other hand, where a child from a minority or low prestige language background is exposed to a high prestige language in the school system, he ends up partly losing competence in his first language while acquiring less than native speaker competence in his second language. This process is referred to as subtractive bilingualism.

2)   High levels of skill in both the spoken and written forms of the native language are necessary for correspondingly high levels of skill in the second language to be achieved. The converse is also true, i.e. low level of competence in the native language will retard the level of competence which could be achieved in the second language.

3)   The cognitive development of children is enhanced by additive bilingualism and retarded by subtractive bilingualism.

The above findings, in the context of the English-lexicon Creole speaking Commonwealth Caribbean, provides support for the view that Creole should function as an official language alongside English. It also supports Carrington's basic position that education has to be provided via the first language of those receiving that education. Ironically, the findings also suggest that the official use of Creole in the education system would improve the level of competence in English in circumstances where '... the teaching of English would ... be an exercise in teaching a new language to an already literate individual.' (Carrington, 1980, p. 187)

The language policy being proposed for the education system, is a bilingual one. Creole would be the initial medium of education, the medium by which literacy is acquired, as well as a subject to be taught. English would be introduced as a second language as early in the education system as is thought sound from an educational standpoint.

The language planning proposals put forward earlier scrupulously avoided the suggestion of a Standard Creole being developed and imposed on the population for official use. The fact that this is not the way we chose to proceed has educational implications. Having acquired the Creole orthography, pupils would be permitted to write in the way that they naturally speak. The time and energy which would be saved in trying to teach pupils to be productive in a new written and spoken Standard Creole could be more profitably spent in aiming at more democratic educational goals. Pupils could be taught to recognise and understand the spoken and written forms of Creole other than those used natively, already exists among many Creole speakers. The school system would try to expand on this knowledge, particularly in the area of written Creole. This particular aspect of Creole language instruction is part of a general tradition in native language instruction which concerns itself with passing on information **about** the language, its varieties, etc.

Conclusion

The solution proposed here is the elevation of Creole to the position of official language. In spite of the emphasis placed on language, it should not be construed that language is the root cause of inequality within the society. Inequality in the area of language is but an expression of the social and economic inequality that exists. However, the fight for people's language rights cannot be postponed until some time in the future when social and economic contradictions disappear. The struggle on the language question is simply one ingredient in the general fight against social and economic injustice.

CHAPTER 7.

Language And Revolutionary Transformation in the Caribbean:
The Case of Guyana

In the previous chapter, we discussed the kind of language reforms which should be implemented in situations where those who favour national liberation have access to state power. The question which arises at this point, however, is what should be done in circumstances where such forces do not control state power. Much of the preceding discussion has been quite general and may have seemed rather abstract. This chapter, therefore, attempts to present a practical programme of how the language problem should be tackled in a specific country, by a mass movement which does not hold state power. The point which is being made there is that the development of appropriate language policies and practices need not, and cannot await acquisition of state power. Language is, after all, the communication medium through which the mass of the population will organise to fight for control of power.

In this chapter, therefore, we will attempt to show how the general theoretical approach developed in previous chapters can be adapted to the specific conditions of a particular country. The case which we will deal with is that of the current language situation in Guyana.

Language as Ideology in Guyana

The ruling class in comtemporary Guyana is made up of a group of people whose origins lie within the educated middle class which developed during the colonial period. The section of this educated middle class which inherited power from the British colonial power at the time of independence, proceeded to use this political power as a means of developing an economic base for itself. Through its control of the machinery of state, this class managed to gain direct control of over 80% of the economy by means of large scale nationalisations in the post-independence period. In a manner so familiar in many ex-colonial countries, the new ruling class has used its monopoly control of the state to dominate almost every area of the society. In these circumstances, the need has arisen to induce among the mass of the population an ideological acceptance of the new social order. The status quo needs to legitimise itself. In order to achieve this, nationalist sentiment and cultural symbols have been heavily manipulated. Language has been used as an important vehicle for asserting ruling class dominance in Guyana, as we shall see.

The exercise of political power in Guyana was, from the time of independence until 1985, heavily concentrated in the hands of one person, Forbes Burnham. Previously Prime Minister and then, with a change in the constitution, President, Burnham throughout his political career, created a popular image of himself as a leader with a high level of competence in English. The implication which this image carried with it is clear. His competence in English, the official language of the country, made him qualified to rule. By contrast, Burnham's main traditional political opponent and present leader of the minority in the parliament, Cheddi Jagan, has been caricatured as having a poor command of 'proper' English. According to this view, Jagan's lack of competence in English serves to disqualify him from holding political power.

The development by the Guyanese ruling class of a mystique around Burnham's ability to use English proceeded in two stages. The first stage was to emphasise to the public at large that Burnham's competence in the Queen's English had received the notice and recognition of the international community, most importantly the English themselves. A quote from Sir Lionel Luckhoo on Burnham's command of spoken English will serve to illustrate this point. He states, '. . . the Prime Minister . . . is a speaker of execellence who won the coveted London University Debate Cup.' (Luckhoo, 1977)

A problem arose, however, with this approach to building up the Burnham language mystique. As the post-independence period progressed, the external and colonialist orientation of this mystique began to clash with the nationalist and even radical image which the regime wished to project. As a result, the build up of the mystique moved to a second stage. The English language usage of prominent members of the new post-colonial ruling class, notably Burnham, was proposed as the model of 'correct' language usage for all Guyanese. (Luckhoo, 1977) In the area of language, as in all other areas of life in Guyana, ruling class power and control have created a ridiculous degree of subservience among those wishing to avoid offending their rulers. For example, one writer of an article to the government-owned *Sunday Chronicle* who describes himself as a handicapped pensioner, has this to say on English language usage in Guyana. '. . . it must be mentioned that there are outstanding people in Guyana worthy of emulation in word usage. President Sampson Burnham is a Titan among our literary men. But can anyone hope to emulate Sampson Burnham?' *(Sunday Chronicle,* April 26, 1981, p. 1, pp. 6-7 Language is such an important prop of the regime in Guyana that those struggling for social change cannot avoid challenging the status quo on the language question.

But what of the attitude of the mass of the population to the language question in Guyana? Rickford (1979, 1983) provides some interesting indications as to the complex nature of language attitudes which exist. Rickford carried out his linguistic research in a village on the East Coast of Demerara which was originally developed as a housing scheme for sugar estate labourers. At the time of the research, however, the village had many inhabitants who could not be described as sugar workers. Twenty-four informants were selected from the community. This group was divided into two sub-groups of twelve. One sub-group of informants was made up of cane-cutters, weeders and other field-workers on the sugar estate. These informants were to represent what Rickford refers to as the Estate Class. The other sub-group was made up of informants who were clerks, contractors, book-keepers and shop-owners. These represented what Rickford calls the Non-Estate Class. He argues that the validity of the distinction between these two socio-economic groups lies in the fact that the Non-Estate Class (NEC) has managed to escape the back-breaking labour, oppressive working conditions and poor pay which remain the lot of the menial estate labourers, i.e. the Estate Class (EC). (Rickford, 1983, p. 5) The informants were each asked to evaluate three speakers via tape recorded samples of their speech. In fact, what appeared to be three speakers were really a single speaker performing in the guise of (i) a basilectal speaker, i.e. a speaker of deep Creole, (ii) a mesolectal speaker, i.e. a speaker of a language variety showing influence from both Creole and English, and (iii) an acrolectal speaker, i.e. a speaker of English.

Informants were given a five-point occupational scale on which to rank the three 'speakers' who they had heard on tape. The scale ranged from cane-cutter, lowest in the prestige hierarchy, to field-manager and headmaster, at the top of the hierarchy. Both the EC and NEC informants in the data agreed in associating basilectal Creole speech with the lowest prestige jobs, acroletal speech with the highest prestige jobs, and mesolectal speech with jobs intermediate on the prestige scale. The informants were also asked to rank the three 'speakers' on a friend scale, i.e. the likelihood of the speaker fitting into the informant's circle of friends. Here, the responses of the EC and NEC informants no longer agree. The NEC informants rate the basilectal Creole speaker at the lowest point on the friend scale, the mesolectal speaker at the highest point on their scale, with the acrolectal speaker getting a rating slightly below that of the mesolectal speaker. The EC informants, on the otheer hand, rated the basilectal speaker at the highest point on their scale, the mesolectal speaker much lower down, with the acrolectal speaker getting the lowest rating of all. (Rickford, 1983, pp. 6-7)

What is the significance of these research findings? Let us first look at the job scale rating. The EC and NEC informants paralleled each other in their ranking of the three 'speakers' along the job scale. However, the motivation behind the ranking by these two sets of informants appears to have been quite different. 92% of the NEC informants believed that speaking English would help them to get a good job and get ahead. However, only 42% of the EC informants held this view. Rickford (1983, pp. 11-12) correctly concludes that whereas the NEC informants saw competence in English as a factor which **contributed** to occupational and social prestige, the EC informants saw competence in English simply as a feature which **reflected** this prestige. This contrast in perception is not surprising. The middle class job functions which the NEC informants perform, in their role as clerks, book-keepers, etc., do require some level of competence in English. On the other hand, for the EC informants members of the rural agricultural working class, use of the official language, English, does not enter into the performance of their job functions. In addition, the EC informants come from a social class within the community which is easily the most exploited and under-privileged. Thus EC informants do not see themselves as being able to move forward via individual acts of self-improvement, e.g. improving their proficiency in English. Rather, as Rickford (1983, p. 12) states, 'It is the **social order** itself which is perceived as in need of change . . . ' All this serves to establish that, among at least some sections of the working class, there has developed a rejection of ruling class domination within the socio-economic system, **as well as** the linguistic order which expresses this domination. Those, therefore, who are involved in politically mobilising the Guyanese working class, ignore the language question at their own peril.

Let us now examine the significance of the results of the friend scale rating. In his analysis of his informants' own language behaviour, Rickford (1983, p. 9) finds that the EC informants use the basilect or deep Creole in their everyday speech, whereas the NEC members of his sample use the mesolect, i.e. varieties in between deep Creole and English. Since the EC informants identified the basilectal speaker on tape as being most likely to become part of their circle of friends, and the NEC informants made the same identification for the mesolectal speaker on tape, there is only one conclusion that can be arrived at. As Rickford

(1983, p. 10) states, the informants responded positively to the speaker on the tape who sounded most like themselves. This positive identification with their own speech, particularly among the basilectal Creole speaking rural working class, goes against the existing stereotype that Creole speakers have a negative attitude to their own speech. Rather, Rickford's findings suggest an extremely positive linguistic self-image among this section of the population. In addition, these findings indicate that use of Creole performs an important role as a symbol of class identity and solidarity among the working class. Political organisation and mobilisation of this class has to involve the conscious and deliberate use of Creole, therefore.

There is a tension between ruling class language values which are imposed on the society, and the language values of the oppressed groups within that society. This is illustrated by the difference in results for the job prestige evaluation as compared with the friendship evaluation. As Rickford (1983, p. 21n) points out, the identification of the job performed by each of the three 'speakers' on tape, reflected conventions imposed on the informants by the society at large. On the other hand, the friendship evaluation reflected values over which the individual informant had some control. The tension between these two sets of value systems often results in ambivalance. For example, Rickford (1979, pp. 95-96) gives 12 examples of informants who, while asserting a positive attitude to Creolese, felt that it was necessary to use English to educated people, to important people, to 'nice people dat talkin proper', to those who do not understand Creolese, etc. It is ironic that, in a society where Creolese is by far the most widely used language variety, monolingual speakers of Creolese would perceive that it is **they** who should make the linguistic adjustment when they come into contact with people from the more privileged sectors of the society.

One of the tasks of political mobilisation in the country has to be to help resolve this ambivalence among the oppressed groups in the community. This means a drastic change in language policy and language practice among those who have taken on the task of politically organising the Guyanese population in the present period of crisis.

What is to be done?

We shall not, here, pay much attention to the kind of official language policy which should be pursued in the event of the mass based parties of the opposition acquiring state power in Guyana. This has already been covered by the discussion in Chapter 6. Rather, we shall consider an outline of the kind of language practices which should be pursued by groups and parties in the

mass movement in the period **before** the acquisition of state
power. Appropriate language policies would (i) help to ensure that
the mass of the population understands the major political issues
and is able to participate fully in the decision-making processes of
the movement, and (ii) encourage linguistic security and language
solidarity among members of the movement, deepening, as a result,
the unity which is being developed.

In Guyana, there is a tendency to associate Africans with the
urban areas and (East) Indians with the countryside. This, however, is a gross over-simplification of the reality. Much modern
work on the language situation in Guyana has fallen into the trap
created by this over-simplification. Thus, Bickerton (1975, p. 211)
refers to a 'rural-Indian/urban African polarisation' which is
supposed to have developed in the country's population distribution. Edwards, in a similar vein, states that '. . . Indians live
predominantly in the rural areas while Blacks and other races are
predominantly urban dwellers.' (Edwards, 1975, p. 77) It would be
sad if plans for the formal use of Creolese within the mass
movement were affected by this stereotype.

The largest ethnic group in the urban centres (Georgetown and
New Amsterdam) is African. In 1970 (Census Research Programme, 1976), 51% of the urban population was African compared with the figure of 26% for Indians in the urban areas.
However, as pointed out by *The American University* (1969, p. 45)
in a comment on the population figures of the late 1960's, the '. . .
urban population is predominantly African, but it is misleading to
suggest that Africans are primarily urban; the majority of the
African population (57 percent) is rural . . .' The percentage of the
African population who, in 1970, lived in the rural areas was 57.5%.
The comparable figure for the Indian population was 87%. Indians,
therefore, turn out to be even more predominantly rural than
Africans. That the two major ethnic groups are predominantly rural
is explained the fact that Guyana is a mainly rural country with 74%
of its population residing outside the towns.

All this has a very serious impact on the first decision which the
mass organisations will have to make on the language question.
This decision involves which variety of Creolese to employ as a
medium of public communication. Edwards (1975), in a detailed
study of Creole language use in Guyana, finds that the urban-rural
factor is the most significant factor affecting language use in the
country. The rural population, both African and Indian, tend to
speak basilectal or 'deep' varieties of Creole, i.e. language showing
relatively little influence from English. The urban population, on
the other hand, he found to be speakers of the mesolect, i.e.
varieties of Creole showing some influence from English. If, based
on the sheer numerical dominance of the rural population, a rural-
based variety of Creole were selected, two problems immediately

appear. One such problem is that, in a society where the race question is a sensitive political issue, this selection might be criticised on grounds that it favours the Indian population. In fact, it would also favour the 57% of the African population who are rural. However, racial chauvinism is usually not based on logic. If the decision were made to select an urban-based variety of Creole, the accusation is likely that Africans are being favoured. This is, of course, in spite of the fact that 57% of the African population would be placed at a disadvantage if such a choice were made.

In spite of the numerical difference between the urban and rural populations in Guyana, the populations are politically of equal importance. The greatest challenge to ruling class power has come when, in 1979 and again in 1983, workers in the state-owned bauxite and sugar industries together were on strike against the economic policies of the government. With the importance of maintaining a balance between the urban and rural population in mind, Devonish (1978) provided a description of a Creole variety which employed syntactic features shared by both urban and rural speakers. This variety, which we will here refer to as Common Creolese, seems to fulfil the linguistic requirements which the mass organisations would have. It would provide a means of communicating with the population in Creolese via a language variety which is not marked as being either urban or rural, but which employs features common to both urban and rural varieties of the language.

Plans for using Creolese formally within mass organisations should proceed in stages. The first stage involves the training of those persons within the organisations who are charged with disseminating information to the public. Such persons, be they writers of pamphlets, journalists, public speakers or political organisers, would need to be made familiar with the structure of Common Creolese. The basic tool for promoting this process of familiarisation would be a normative description of Common Creolese. Such a description would, of course, have to be prepared for this purpose. This familiarisation would include learning a standard writing system for Creolese, very probably a modified version of the Cassidy writing system developed for Jamaican Creole.

In this process of familiarising key people with Common Creolese, it will be important to stress the precise role it is expected to perform. It would be the language medium by which the mass organisations could communicate most effectively with the widest cross-section of the population possible. It would also perform another function. Many of the disseminators of information, although perhaps speakers of Creolese in private informal situations, are likely to find difficulty in using Creolese as a public formal language. In spite of themselves, their efforts to use Creolese in public formal situations are likely to show so much English interference as to make the whole exercise meaningless. Common Creolese, therefore, provides a model off of which such persons can consciously pattern their language usage in the new situations where Creolese is required. Common Creolese, however, is not a language variety which should be imposed on the Creolese speaking population as a standard. Rather, I propose that it function as a catalyst for bringing about a general realisation that Creolese can perform all the communicative functions which exists within the society. Based on this new linguistic self-awareness, the mass organisations would encourage speakers of Creolese to use their **own** varieties of the language in their contact with, or participation in these organisations. People would also be encouraged to write in their own varieties of Creolese, using the writing system developed for the language. Common Creolese would, therefore, simply be a means of encouraging all the varieties of Creolese in the speech community to blossom forth.

Having made disseminators of information familiar with Common Creolese and its intended functions, the next stage would be to explain to the population what is being attempted and why. Public education on the language question is not going to occur over-night, and there is likely to be long and heated argument on the correctness or otherwise of the language practices being implemented. In the case of Creolese usage in the print medium, an additional stage has to precede the implementation of the new practices. In the newspapers, pamphlets and other publications produced by the mass organisations, space would need to be devoted to introducing the Creolese orthography to the readership, and teaching it to them. It is only as the familiarity of the readership with the orthography increases, that the transition from using English to using Creolese in these publications can take place.

The set of language practices being proposed here for mass organisations in Guyana, involves the spread of Creolese into domains where it has not previously functioned. The question then arises of how the linguistic resources of the language are to be expanded in order for it to perform its new functions as a formal language medium for discussing political and economic issues. It is this matter that we will look at in some detail in the next section.

How it is to be done

How does one go about expanding the linguistic resources of Creolese in order for it to adequately perform its new functions? This we will find out by looking at a concrete example. What follows is (i) a Creolese translation of a piece of political discourse, (ii) a literal English translation of the Creolese passage, and (iii) the original English passage. These form the basis for the discussion of how what is to be done is to be done.

A. The Creolese Version

(1) Hóu di partii wa ruulin get in powa? (2) A set a big shat wid monii, som from insaid di kontrii an som from awee, mek bargin wid di partii wa ruulin nou, an put it in powa. (3) Baps, 1970 and 1971 kom, an di govament staat tek-ova nof big biznis. (4) Nof badii stan op an wach dis an taak se hou di govament gaan pon di püpl said an ton geens outsaid kontrool. (5) Gi Jak hii jakit. (6) Di tek-ova ting bin gud fo di Gainiiz piil. (7) Bot arinj yala, da na se ii switt. (8) Yu sii di big kompanii-dem awee wa bin oon di kompanii-dem wa tek-ova? (9) Di govament gat di kontrii pee-in truu it tiit fo pee aaf di püpl outsaid fo wa tek. (10) Pon tap a da, di govament kiip aan, jos laik lang taim, baiin an selin wid di seem set a rich kontrii we wan wan püpl lak aaf di laiyan sheer a wa projuus. (11) Plos, di govament bai-in mashiin an ting from dem seem kontrii, an den gat fo ton rong an pee di seem püpl fo di sapii fo wok di mashiin-dem. (12)Iz dem ting-dis wa mek püpl kech deself an sii di truut. (13) Lang taim, dem wa de in govament nou bin a set a poo-greet püpl wa een bin oon wan ting. (14) Nou, truu di govament, dem oon an kontrool nof. (15) Aal a dem ton from biis to priis. (16) Wa dem nou oon an kontrool gii dem stregk fo hool aan pon govament powa mo strang, an spred out dem powa moo.

B. The English Literal Translation

(1) How did the ruling party get into power? (2) A set of big-shots with money, some from inside the country and some from outside, made a deal with the present ruling party, and put it in power. (3) Then 1970 and 1971 came, and the government started to take over many large businesses. (4) Many people stood up, watched this, and said that the government had moved unto the side of the people and had turned against outside control. (5) Give Jack his jacket (6) The take-over thing (the nationalisations) was good for the Guyanese people. (7) But the fact that an orange is yellow does not necessarily mean that it is sweet. (8) You see the big companies abroad which owned the companies which were taken over? (9) The government has the country paying through its teeth to pay off the foreigners for what was taken over. (10) On top of that, the government has kept on just as before, buying from and selling to the same set of rich countries where only a few people appropriate for themselves the lion's share of what is produced. (11) In addition, the government is buying machines and such like from those same countries, and have to turn around and pay the same people for the know-how to operate the machinery. (12) It is things like this which have made people wake up and see the truth. (13) In days gone by, those who are presently in government were a set of petty bourgeois who owned nothing. (14) Now, through the government, they own and control a great deal. (15) They have a

turned from beasts into priests. (16) What they now own and control have given them the ability to hold on to government power even more strongly, and to extend that power further.

C. The Original Passage

Because the ruling party came to power in alliance with both local and foreign capital, analyses of developments since the beginning of its nationalisation drive in 1970/71 typically refer to its "leftward swing to anti-imperialism". In effect, however, while nationalisation was an objectively progressive step for the country, its roots in heavy compensation for the foreign owners and unchanged trade, marketing and technology arrangements with the capitalist world, provided the first indications that state control of the economy was aimed at creating an economic base for an essentially non-owning petty bourgeois ruling class, and on that base, the potential for the consolidation and expansion of its political power.
(Working People's Alliance, 1979, pp. 5-6)

Passage C is written in a particularly dense style, with several propositions being compressed into two extremely long sentences. It contains certain specialised terminology such as 'leftward', 'anti-imperialism', 'petty bourgeois', 'progressive' and 'objectively', typical of left-wing political writing in English. In order for the passage to be translated adequately, the style of the passage has to be drastically altered to correspond with normal Creolese discourse style. As for the specialised terminology, it would not be satisfactory to simply borrow these from English. These terms would be totally unfamiliar to monolingual speakers of Creolese, and thus the whole point of using Creolese for this kind of discourse would be partly defeated. If socialist and Marxist analysis is going to become an integral part of the popular culture, specialised terminology will have to be generated within the linguistic and cultural universe of the people. According to Walter Rodney. 'You have to see with the eyes of the people. You have to hear with the ears of the people. You have to speak with the voice of the people.' (Rodney, 1979) This is what the Creolese version in Passage A attempts to achieve.

Passage A (the Creolese version) is made up of 16 sentences as compared with the 2 sentences of Passage C (the English original). What the Creolese passage does is to separate into distinct sentences the several propositions which are crammed into the two sentences of the English original. This produced a passage which was much more in line with the normal Creolese discourse structure. In spite, however, of the great discrepancy in the number of sentences in two passages, Passage A with 21 lines is only 1.75 times as long as Passage C with 12 lines.

One of the effects of the number of sentences used in Passage A, was to create a need for linking and transition devices between the the sentences. Simple but careful juxtaposition of sentences was use in the majority of cases. However, in Sentence 3, the word 'baps' was used to introduce the sentence. The word is, in origin, an onomatpoeia used for signalling a sudden or unexpected event. It is therefore employed in Sentence 3 to introduce information which would be unexpected in the light of what was said in Sentence 2. Where it is necessary to provide a listing of information across a series of sentences, forms such as 'pon tap a da' (Sentence 10) and 'plos' (Sentence 11) were used.

Creolese has been traditionally used only as an oral medium of communication. If written Creolese of the type attempted in Passage A is not to appear stilted and artificial, some features of oral Creolese usage have to be retained in the new medium. It is for this reason that both the first sentence of Passage A and a sentence towards the middle (Sentence 8) are rhetorical questions. The aim is to keep a quasi-oral interaction going between writer and reader. As part of the attempt to retain a strong oral element in the Creolese translation, a Creolese proverb is employed in Sentence 7, and an idiomatic expression in Sentence 15. Neither of these add new information to the text. In Sentence 7, what the proverb does is to act as a link between the positive piece of information conveyed in the previous sentence and the negative information to come in the next few sentences. In the case of Sentence 15, the idiom merely serves to sum up neatly what has already been said in the previous two sentences. In contrast to the use to which traditional Creolese expressions have been put in Sentences 7 and 15, in Sentence 5, the proverb 'Gi Jak hii jakit' is used as a translation for the word 'objectively' in the original English passage. This particular proverb is used in conversation as an injunction to be fair even to those one does not like, i.e. give the devil his due. This proverb, therefore, contains the essence of what is expressed by the English word 'objectively'.

This brings us to the question of translation of the specialised terminology in the original passage. One device which was resorted to was circumlocution. For example, the term 'capitalist world' in the English original was translated as 'di ... set a rich knotrii we war piipl lak aaf di laiyan sheer a wa projuus.' (Sentence 10) This circumlocution has stuck very close to the meaning of the term 'capitalist world' as used in the English original. A different approach had to be taken in dealing with the term 'local and foreign capital'. A careful reading of the first sentence of Passage C indicates that what is really meant is 'capitalists' rather than 'capital'. The Creolese translation for 'capitalists' is *a set a big sha wid monii.* (Sentence 2) this particular circumlocution is a bit more general that the English term 'capitalists'. There are people who have lots of money but who are not capitalists in the strict sense of the word. However, it was felt that in the context of the passage being translated, a narrower, more precise and much longer circumlocution was unnecessary.

Dealing with 'anti-imperialism' initially looked formidable. However, after identifying *'outsaid kontrool'* as the Creolese translation for 'imperialism', then 'anti-imperialism' would naturally be a position *'geens outsaid knotrool'* i.e. against outside control. (Sentence 4) The term 'leftward' referring to the political outlook of individuals, presented a much more serious problem. The description of politics in terms of left and right is purely a matter of European linguistic convention. It owes its origin to the sides of the French National Assembly on which members of opposing factions sat during the 19th century. The alternative selected was to divide up the political spectrum in Creolese into those *'pon di piipl said'* i.e. on the side of the people (Sentence 4) and those *'geens di püpl'*. It may be argued that such a division is not objective. I do not claim that it is. Neither is the traditional terminology which ends up associating the political 'right' with that which is right, i.e. correct. In favour of the division which I propose, it could be argued that making a basic political distinction between those on the side of the people and those who are not, would be a fairly profound way of stimulating political discourse in Creolese.

Translating 'trade' as *'bai-in an selin'* i.e. buying and selling (Sentence 10) presented no problem. Neither did the translation of 'technology arrangements', presumably the purchase of technological know-how, which was translated as the purchase of *'sapii fo wok di mashiin-dem'*. i.e. the knowledge to operate the machines. (Sentence 11) As for 'nationalisation', this was translated as *'tek-ova'*. (Sentence 3, 5) This translation has a distinct advantage over its English equivalent. 'Nationalisation' suggests the idea of making something the property of the nation. There is some contradiction, therefore, in suggesting that nationalisations that have taken place in places like Guyana have not placed control of nationalised property into the hands of the nation but into the hands of a tiny elite. With the Creolese term *'tek-ova'*, anybody can take over property, the government, an elite, or the nation.

There was one case, where, in doing the translation, I was forced to tamper with the linguistic resurces of Creolese. This involved finding an equivalent for the English term 'petty bourgeois'. The term which I use, *'poo-greet'* (Sentence 13) is normally used to refer to poor people with what might be called petty bourgeois aspirations. It is, in its usual sense, descriptive of a social attitude rather than a class position. I have extended the meaning of the term to cover a class of people who, like the working class, are non-property-owning, but who find themselves in the privileged position of acting as intermediaries between the working class and peasantry, on one hand, and the ruling class, on the other.

Conclusion

This chapter has attempted to demonstrate the necessity of tackling the Creole language problem, even in those cases where the organisations and parties concerned do not form part of the government of the country. Additionally, an effort has been made to show that alternative language policies and practices are a practical proposition in such situations. When, however, the linguistic status quo is not questioned in the period before state power is achieved, it becomes extremely difficult, when in power, to come to terms with the language question. This is demomstrated by the case of the Grenadian Revolution which will be the focus of the concluding chapter.

CHAPTER 8.

National Liberation and the Creole Language Question: A Conclusion

How has the Creole language question been handled when state power comes into the hands of those committed to the principle of national liberation? It is this question which this chapter sets out to answer. The experiences of these political processes can teach us some very sobering lessons. The chapter will, in passing, touch the Creole language question as it has been dealt with by the Sandinista government of Nicaragua. After the revolution in 1979, the Nicaraguan government had to deal with linguistic minorities, notably that of the English-lexicon Creole speaking minority on the Miskita Coast. The major focus of this chapter, however, will be on Grenada and on the language policies and practices of the People's Revolutionary Government (P.R.G.) and the New Jewel Movement (N.J.M.) during the Grenedian Revolution, from 1979-1983. It is perhaps fitting that this work should end with a focus on Grenada. The original idea of writing a work such as this was born out of frustration at the failure of the Grenadian government to even contemplate appropriate measures on the language question after the 1979 revolution.

The Nicaraguan Experience

The Sandinistas who seized power in Nicaragua were committed to a national campaign to wipe out illiteracy. In addition to the large Spanish-speaking majority of the population, there were linguistic minorities that also had to be drawn into the literacy crusade. One of these minorities were speakers of Miskita Coast Creole, an English-lexicon Creole. According to Robert Pring-Mill (personal communication) who visited the Miskita Coast in the period after the revolution, there was a very serious debate about whether to use English or Creole as the medium for teaching literacy. Interestingly enough, the more privileged sectors of the Miskita Coast population, who had had access to education in English, supported the idea of literacy being taught in Creole. For these persons, a mass literacy campaign in the area in English would erode the special privilege they had of having access to a prestigious international language. Understandably, the monolingual

Creole-speaking majority accepted the view of the privileged minority that the purpose of literacy acquisition was to allow access to English. The result was that, in the name of equality, the demand came from the monolingual Creole-speaking community that literacy should be taught in English. The revolutionary process had had relatively little support in the area and those in charge of the literacy programme seemed to have decided to go along with the wishes of the population. Obviously, through lack of political direction and a failure to understand what literacy skills involve, these Creole-speakers were consenting to the devaluation of any literacy skills which they did acquire. Having no command of English, they would have been unable to read or write in that language. They had made this choice rather than opt for literacy in their native language along with an expansion of the roles and functions of Creole in the area.

In all this, Nicaragua sought assistance from revolutionary Grenada. As we shall see, Grenada had not itself come to terms with its own Creole language problem. It too had taken the apparently easy option of teaching literacy in English. As a result, the Grenadian assistance only confirmed the Nicaraguan literacy crusade in the decision which had already been taken. The assistance mainly took the form of two teachers from Grenada's own mass literacy campaign going to do literacy work on the Miskita Coast of Nicaragua. (EPICA Task Force, 1982, p. 84)

Official Attitudes to Language in Revolutionary Grenada

In a paper submitted by the Women's Desk, an organ of the Grenadian government, to the National Seminar on Education in July, 1979, it is stated that 'Dialect was forced upon us due to our denial of education in society in the early days'. (*Women's Desk,* 1979, p. 3) the implication behind this statement was that, with the advent of the revolution and the access to education which would follow, Grenadian Creole could and should be wiped out. Fortunately, this was not a position generally shared by those directly wielding political power in the country. It nevertheless represented a distinctly unrevolutionary attitude to language, the fact that it was clothed in revolutionary rhetoric notwithstanding.

A more sophisticated version of the same position can be seen in a statement by the then head of the Grenedian government, Maurice Bishop. 'If all our people are able at least at a minimum level to read and write . . . It will be so much easier for them to understand this word we use so often, that we call *Imperialism.* It will be so much easier for them to understand what we mean when we talk of *destabilisation,* what we mean when we say that the Revolution is for the people, and that the people *are* the Revolution.' (Bishop, 1984, p. 58) (emphasis in the original) At first glance, the above statement does not make sense. What does teaching people to read and write have to do with them being able to understand when certain words or sentences are produced in speech? An appreciation of the socio-linguistic situation does provide some help. English is the only language normally used in writing in Grenada. Therefore, acquiring literacy implies the acquisition of some amount of English. Since the normal language of public political discourse is also English, a knowledge of English would enable people to understand political speeches. Since the political leadership of the Grenadian Revolution had all received some level of formal education, available, of course, only in English, the attitude being expressed by Bishop was one of 'they (the masses) must learn our language (English)'.

There was, however, another more democratic line of thinking on the language question. With reference to the discipline of Economics, Bernard Coard, the Deputy Prime Minister and Minister of Finance states, '... we are caught up in a situation where individuals among our people went to universities not only to advance themselves intellectually and academically, but also, whether consciously or unconsciously, to acquire an entire mould of thinking, writing and speaking that becomes incomprehensible to the vast majority of the people... When an economist talks you are supposed to be blinded by science, and the language and terminology is such as to haev the population bewildered, bemused, confused and either thinking the whole thing is a waste of time or totally accepting it all whether it makes sense or not.' (cited in Searle, 1984, pp. 95-96) Coard goes on to outline in great detail the institutional arrangements made for allowing mass participation in the formulation of the National Budget. These arrangements took the form of a National Conference on the Economy followed by discussions at Parish and Zonal Council levels. However, he makes no statement on what should be done about language. While conscious of the language problem, Coard seems unaware of what could or should be done about it. The result was, quite naturally, the presentation of the original budget proposals to these groups of citizens in English, albeit accompanied by explanations, and in the most non-technical language possible. Thus, even though the spirit of this approach is one of 'we (the leadership) should speak their language (Creole)', the actual language practice it produced was not significantly different from that inspired by the 'they must learn our language' approach.

These differences in position often existed within the same individuals speaking at different times. It would, therefore, be quite incorrect to suggest that such differences had anything to do with the leadership crisis which developed in September/October, 1983. When these two contradictory positions on the language question were combined with the increase in national pride and self-confidence stimulated by the revolution, there was only one likely outcome, officially sanctioned diglossia. Such a diglossia is very common elsewhere in the Commonwealth Caribbean. The coming together of the various strands of opinion on the language question is best expressed by Chris de Riggs, poet and Minister of Health in the P.R.G. He states, 'We need Standard English as an international instrument and for study, newspapers and radio, but we would be culturally incomplete, we wouldn't be even standing on one leg, if we couldn't understand and use our dialect..' (in Searle, 1984, p. 130) This 'can't stand on one leg' view was the typical official position.

Bilingualism is a term that cropped up very frequently in official statements. The description of Grenada as a bilingual country, in which both Creole and English are used, seems on the surface to involve quite an important concession to Creole-speakers and their language. However, in a country with a truly bilingual official language policy, an attempt is made to provide access to all areas of national life in each of the two languages. What de Riggs in the quote above is suggesting is that it is acceptable to have a system of language use at the national level which excludes monolingual Creole-speakers from being able to study, read newspapers or listen to the radio. What was being actively promoted was not true bilingualism but diglossia. According to an introductory document on language arts in the primary school which was distributed to all teachers, '... There need be no rivalry between the two languages, as each has it (sic) own very important functions ... The two forms of expression complement each other ... Neither can replace the other.' (cited in Searle, 1984, p. 72) Implicit in this is an acceptance of the linguistic status quo as inherited from the period before the revolution. This situation was one in which English operated as the official, public-formal and sole written language variety in the country. Creole was the language variety used as a means of everyday informal communication among the mass of the population. These two language varieties complemented each other in the same way as do the rich man in his castle and the poor man at his gate, each with his estate clearly ordered.

What then had changed as a result of the revolution in Grenada? Traditionally, no concession had been made to the existence of any language variety other than English. Creole was simply regarded as 'broken English', a bastard form of speech possessing no rules, and Grenada was therefore considered a monolingual English-speaking country. The revolution helped create some recognition of Creole as a separate linguistic system from English. This had the effect of encouraging the official image of Grenada as, in some sense, a bilingual rather than monolingual country. There had been a change in labelling. This was certainly an advance, placing Grenada alongside countries like Jamaica and Guyana, in which some degree of official recognition exists that two linguistic systems coexist within the society. What did not change in Grenada or elsewhere, were the roles and functions performed by the two language varieties. The rhetoric was now more nationalist on the Creole language question, but little had changed for monolingual Creole-speakers who continued to find themselves excluded from many areas of national life by virtue of their lack of competence in English.

Official Language Policies in Grenada

As we have already seen in previous chapters, it is usually the education system which becomes the major focus of debate on the Creole language question. In those countries of the Commonwealth Caribbean in which an English-lexicon Creole is widely spoken, the education system is often the only area in which an explicit official language policy emerges. Grenada proved no exception to the general trend. After the revolution in March, 1979, a series of national consultations were held on the question of education reform. At the National Seminar on Education in July, 1979, two sets of proposals (Devonish, 1979; Kephart, 1979) on the language question were made. The gist of these proposals was that a standard writing system for Grenadian English-lexicon Creole be developed. This would be accompanied by the granting of official status to Creole in the society at large and, more specifically, within the education system. The participants in the National Seminar, mostly teachers, were split almost in half over whether such proposals were relevant and whether Grenada did indeed have a language problem. One reason for such strong opposition lay in the fact that unlike issues of economic policy, social equality, etc., the language question had never been raised as part of the political debate in the country. Apart from the negative reaction of those who instinctively wished to defend the linguistic status quo, there were many who sympathised with the proposals but who could not imagine how it would work in practice. At this point, these proposals died a natural death. They had no impact on official thinking, notably on the issue of the role of language in the education system.

The ideas behind these proposal did not disappear, however. In late 1982, Kephart, a former United States Peace Corps Volunteer in Carriacou, returned to carry out an experiment in teaching Creole-speaking children to read and write in their native language. He devised a phonemically based writing system for this purpose. The project had both a negative and positive aim. On the negative side, Kephart wished to establish that acquiring literacy in Creole would not damage the ability of children to read and write English. Many of those who oppose literacy teaching in Creole claim that damage would be done to competence in English. On the positive side, he wished to demonstrate that acquisition of literacy skills in the first language of the children would actually improve their literacy skills in English.

Using a group of 12 year old children from Carriacou Junior Secondary School who were identified by their teachers as being unable to read English, Kephart set about his task. In the course of the year long exercise, it was established that acquiring literacy in Creole did not damage what little literacy skills they already had in English. Rather, the trend seemed to be one in which literacy skills in English improved alongside the development of literacy in Creole. However, the experiment was interrupted by the events surrounding the arrest and eventual murder of Prime Minister Maurice Bishop, and the subsequent U.S. invasion of Grenada. The project eventually came to a premature end. As a result, the findings of Kephart's analysis of his experiment do not allow him to arrive at precise and definite conclusions. At a level more general than that of his experimental group, however, Kephart makes some very telling observations. Persons already literate in English were quite enthusiastic about seeing their language written, and in a phonemically based writing system. They seemed to have little difficulty in learning the writing system after a brief period of exposure to it. (Kephart, 1984a; 1984b)

Meanwhile, as far as I can find out, those persons with a political responsibility for the Ministry of Education remained completely unaware of the work Kephart was doing. The same seems to be true of the senior officials within that Ministry. As with the 1979 proposals at the National Seminar of Education, those in charge were looking the other way. They were too involved in their own programme of reproducing diglossia under the guise of promoting bilingualism. The official position on the language question within the education system is best expressed by the following quotation from a document entitled 'Language Arts in the Primary School'. 'Language Arts teaching no longer aims at erasing our first language and replacing it by the official language, but at **adding another language** to our repertoire, in our case International English. The educated West Indian is bilingual.' (in Searle, 1984, pp. 72-73) (emphasis in the original) The document goes on to state that Language Arts teaching does not mean the teaching of English. Rather, it means the teaching of language skills '. . . which can be developed to begin with in the child's first language and transferred to the target language as the child gains mastery of the latter.' (p. 73)

Hidden behind this apparently liberal approach is the view that Creole is only a medium to be used 'to begin with', and that having transferred whatever skills have been developed to the 'target' the child's language skills in his native language need no further development. This position flows logically from an acceptance of the prevailing diglossic situation in which use of Creole was restricted to private, informal and non-written modes of communication. The pupil could be presumed to develop Creole language skills in these areas in the course of their normal social exposure. The task of the School was to provide language skills in the 'target' language, the language used in public, formal and written comunication. The pupil was being trained to fit into the existing diglossia. The elements from the educated sectors of the population who largely made up the political leadership of the revolution, were whether they realised it not, setting up an education system designed to reproduce themselves and their language behaviour. Such persons, having either themselves come from Creole-speaking language backgrounds or having had considerablee exposure to Creole in the course of their social interaction, would have tended to use some variety of Creole in their private informal interaction. However, when it comes to any topic involving information directly acquired through the education system, in formal situations or via the written word, considerable difficulty existed in such persons trying to communicate in Creole. Ironically, the more education such people have, and therefore the more information they have which should be of relevance to monlingual Creole speakers, the more difficult it becomes to communicate such information in Creole. The reason is, of course, that English is the language in which all such information would have been acquired.

The language education policies developed in Grenada during the period of the revolution do not differ in any way to those which were emerged in Jamaica, Guyana and Trinidad and Tobago in recent years and which were discussed in Chapter 5. The result of such policies, in the form of the *Marryshow Readers* for primary schools, are also the same. The criticisms levelled at the *Jamaican Primary Language Arts* course in Chapter 5, seem largely applicable to the Grenadian course, basing as I do my conclusions on a description of the course by Merle Hodge, one of its designers. (in Searle, 1984, pp. 78-82)

The leadership of the Grenadian Revolution expressed a public commitment to the principle of popular democracy and mass participation in the process of national decision-making. Because, however, they did not question the existing linguistic order, their analysis was that the main barrier to mass participation was one of lack of education, and, in particular, a low level of literacy. This explains why, in the quote from Bishop cited above, it was felt that literacy teaching was an answer to the problem of ordinary people not understanding the meaning of 'imperialism' and 'destabilisation'. According to Valerie Cornwall, the National Co-ordinator of the *Centre for Popular Education* (C.P.E.), 'We wanted to put literacy skills into their correct perspective, so that with them our people could use them for a twofold purpose. Firstly to obtain information, and then by expressing themselves about the reality they now understand, move towards changing that same reality.' (in Searle, 1984, p. 57) In spite of this commitment to communicating with the mass of the population, Cornwall expresses a strong attachment to the existing diglossia when she states, 'We recognise that Standard English is essential to us, and is the medium through which we read and write and express ourselves in certain formal situations. But our people speak Creole everyday of their lives.' (in Searle, 1984, p. 58) Note that whether intentionally or not, the 'we' and 'us' in the above refers to the English-speaking educated elite. On the other hand, the term 'our people' is extended patronisingly to describe uneducated Creole speakers.

The *Centre for Popular Education* (C.P.E.) was established after the revolution, was an adult education programme. The first phase of this programme was a mass literacy campaign. As one would expect from the approach of the political leadership to the question of communication with the public, it was literacy in English which was taught. The philosophy and design of the C.P.E. programme was strongly influenced by the work of the Brazilian educator, Paulo Freire, and by the experience of the mass literacy programme in Cuba in the period after the revolution in that country. The fact is, however, that the bulk of Freire's experiences teaching literacy involved apparently monolingual speech communities in countries such as Brazil and Chile. (Freire, 1970, 1972, 1973) In the case of Cuba as well, what was involved was a largely monolingual Spanish-speaking speech community.

Neither of the two influences pointed in the direction of the C.P.E. needing to come to terms with a language problem, or at least so it seems on the surface. However, a reading of Freire (1978, p. 127) shows that when confronted with the Portugese-lexicon Creoles of Cape Verde and Guinea-Bassau, he immediately recognised that attempts to teach literacy in Portugese to speakers of these languages constituted a serious pedagogical problem. He went so far as to suggest that the Creole of Guinea-Bissau be standardised and given the status of a national language. This particular work by Friere was in the possession of the politicians and technical staff involved in the setting up of the C.P.E. literacy campaign. The Cuban experience as well involved some problems with the Creole language question. Thus, after the declaration of a national war on illiteracy in Cuba in April, 1961, only 3.9% of the adult population remained illiterate by the end of the year. 'A large proportion of the 3.0 percent . . . consisted of blind, deaf, and institutionalized people difficult to reach through conventional literacy means, and also some 25,000 Haitian sugarcane cutters who spoke Creole.' (Arnove, 1981, p. 244n)

In the fact of all this, the failure to deal with the Creole language question, even at the level of the C.P.E. was either a case of the grossest criminal negligence or was deliberate. Inevitably, of course, problems arose. According one report, '. . . there were certain pedagogical problems unique to Grenada which could only be solved by West Indian technicians and teachers through trial and error.' (*EPICA Task Force*, 1982, p. 82) Although not specifically stated, the language question must have figured high among these pedagogical problems. When, in September, 1983, the Central Committee of the N.J.M. concluded that both the party and the revolution were in danger of collapse, views were expressed that not enough C.P.E. work was being done in the army or through the party. (*N.J.M. Central Committee Minutes*, 14-16 September 1983, p. 9) In terms of N.J.M. party jargon, what was meant was that the political message of the party was not reaching the various sectors concerned. Yet, even at that late stage and in the considerable state of desperation about the predicted collapse of the revolutionary process, the language question was never raised.

Language Practices

As we pointed out in the previous section, the education process occurring as it does in English, linguistically alienates those being educated from the monolingual Creole-speakers who make up the majority of the population. This alienation would have applied to the bulk of the political leadership, most of whom had at least secondary education in a society where such education was a special privilege for a tiny minority. Since this leadership would have acquired the bulk of its information about politics in English, it is not surprising that this alienation showed itself in political speeches, even those in which the speaker is attempting to use some Creole. For example, in speeches by Maurice Bishop (in Searle, 1984, pp. 111-112, p. 113, pp. 114-116), the analogies about the yard fowl, cricket and sitting down with the wife to discuss how to budget for the week, all are produced in Creole albeit with some grammatical interference from English. However almost invariably, it is clear that Creole is being used for stylistic purposes. When the normal unmarked style of delivery occurs, notably in introducing issues and drawing conclusions, English is employed. Thus, even within a speech given by a single person in a given situation, evidence of diglossia appears. Each language has its own range of stylistic and topic functions. The use of Creole for abuse, humour and describing domestic relations simply reinforces the inferior position of Creole within the diglossia.

An example of the kind of linguistic alienation existing between the Creole-speaking mass of the population and the leadership educated in English, can be seen in the notes of a soldier of the

People's Revolutionary Army (P.R.A.) presented in O'Shaughnessy (1984, pp. 10-11) which I cite, without any alteration.

Camp Fedon Topic 25 February 17th 1980

The need for Political Concousness

*In our New Revolutionary Army or high level of Political and
revolutionary Awareness is a defnite Measure of the Readiness of the
soldier to defend the homeland and the Rev the soldiers who is
concous of the Arms of the Revolution who is july aware that his is
upholding the Power of the Working People that he and others
defending a cause whose victory means a better way of high for this
Justice generation is the soldier who will give his life to the homeland,
in the firm believe that he as made the most contribution of the Revo
imperilist foreign donation of our enemy and explatation of Rasoway,
e.g. cocoa, nutmeg, banana*
*Revolutionary Army Remember that you are champions of the
intreast of the Workers and Peasesentry a defender of the Peoples
some of the great Revolution Worker and Pleassent it is your duty to
set a fine example of the Revolutioni concouness you should be the
first to engage the enemy and the last to rest similarly you should set
an example of the Revolutionary and this is to courage And Discipline
it is you sacred duty to maintan a spirit of comradeship cohesion and
solidary in the Ranks of the PRA*
We must see our selves as soldiers
Ready to die in the defence of the homeland and of socialism

This was cited by O'Shaughnessy (1984, p. 10) as an example of the
high quality of political attitudes and morale in the PRA as early as
within the first year of its establishment. The soldier has obvious
problems handling the conventions of written English. This does
not concern us, except to observe that the absence of punctuation
suggests that the soldier would have had great difficulty reading
those notes and making much sense of them. We are much more
interested in the how much he understood of what was obviously a
political lecture given in English by a political or military leader.
The extremely deviant spellings for 'peasant' (Pleassent), 'peasantry' (Peasesentry) and 'domination' (donation) suggest complete unfamiliarity with the way these words are even pronouced in
English. At the same time, none of these spellings can be explained
by any phonological adaptation into the pronunciation system of
Grenadian Creole. It is therefore reasonable to conclude that the
soldier is unlikely to have known the meanings of these words in
English. In the eighth line of the notes, there is a stretch '. . . a better

way of high for this generation . . .' which so clearly does not make sense as to suggest that the soldier was simply writing down words as he heard them, with no grasp of the syntactic relations between them. While some element of the political or military leadership was sprouting a stream of left-wing terminology in English, all under the guise of 'politically educating' the army, what the ordinary solidier understood can be seen from the notes.

Alienation involving language was not, however, restricted to communication with the 'masses'. Within the N.J.M. party structure itself, there were differences in levels of formal education which affected competence in English. For example, the note-taker at the Central Committee Meeting of the N.J.M. on 14-16 September, 1983, appears to have problems in writing English which were caused by lack of familiarity with the language. There were problems of agreement of subject and verb, absence of **-ed** type verb inflections, non-use of - **s** in nouns with generic meanings, all a direct result of Creole language interference. There was, as well, a certain amount of hypercorrection. None of these problems, however, seriously interfered with communication.

On the question of language use by members of the Central Committee itself, the highest decision-making body in revolutionary Grenada, the minutes of the meeting of 14-16 September, 1983, provide some interesting clues. It is sometimes difficult to identify when un-English forms crop up in the minutes because of the note-taker himself, or because he ends up writing exactly what was said. It is, however, very likely that a considerable amount of Creole was used in Central Committee discussions. Such Creole use was, however, often heavily weighted down with loan words from English, as in example (1) below. In addition, the minutes suggest that certain 'fancy' English words and sentence structures were being used with meanings very different from those which they would normally bear in English. Examples (2) and (3) provide examples of this. In example (3), the Central Committee member is arguing that his time is wasted in his post as Ambassador to Cuba since links with that country are being pursued through channels other than the Ambassador. Example (4) is an illustration of the very frequent use of apparently 'scientific' left-wing terminology in a manner which seems totally meaningless. The examples are taken from the Central Committee Minutes of 14-16 September, 1983.

1) 'He said that the C.C. continue to be loose and disorganise and unfocus, . . . ' (p. 17)

2) 'He said that if this concensus is widespread . . .' (p. 23)

3) '. . . but he feels that his time is seriously wasted as

Ambassador to Cuba because the work is carried out inspite
of him.' (p. 24)

4)   'Our situation requires tactical objective strategy.' (p. 28)

It is ironic, in the light of example (4), that Searle (1984, p. 105)
described the bombastic form of English used by Eric Gairy, the
former Prime Minister who had been deposed in 1979, as '. . . a
grotesque charade of words to lay smoke screens over the suffering
of the people.'

A feeling which I have developed from a reading of some of
N.J.M. Central Committee minutes is that some members did not
entirely understand the meanings of certain technical political
terms which they were using. It may be, therefore, that, at the very
highest levels of the political leadership in Grenada, there were
some persons with language related problems. For such individuals, their grasp of political issues would have suffered from the
fact that they had not learnt their political analysis in their native
language. From the preceding discussion, it is possible to construct
a diagram which would illustrate the nature of the communication
that was taking place, the symbol —> represents communication
taking place without significant language problems -/-> represents
communication blocked or seriously hampered by such problems.
And -?-> represents an intermediate case involving only partial
communication problems. Our concern is with the communication
on political matters and issues related to the governing of the
country.

PEOPLE	--->	LEADERS	(speech)
PEOPLE	--/-->	LEADERS	(writing)
LEADERS	--/-->	PEOPLE	(speech)
LEADERS	--/-->	PEOPLE	(writing)
PEOPLE	---->	PEOPLE	(speech)
PEOPLE	--/-->	PEOPLE	(writing)
LEADERS	--?-->	LEADERS	(speech)
LEADERS	--?-->	LEADERS	(writing)

Creole-speakers who wished to speak in their native language could
communicate with the leadership. Since the latter were either from
Creole-speaking backgrounds themselves or had had considerable
exposure to the language in the ocurse of their social interaction,
communication would have taken place. In addition, within the

Creole-speaking population itself, there would have been no language barrier to spoken communication. However, the society was diglossic. As a result, all forms of writing apart from some poetry and folk-type literary works, had to be in English. Another effect of diglossia was to force all diglossic persons, i.e. those persons with some level of competence in the high-prestige language, to use it when communicating in speech on 'serious' topics such as politics. A result of this diglossia was that Creole speakers who had a limited command of English were largely excluded from communication or being communicated with in writing. Diglossia also meant that the leadership was prevented from communicating effectively in speech, since only English could be used. And, within the leadership itself, for those whose competence in English was limited, some language problems did exist for communicating or being communicated with on political issues.

Conclusion

Many sections of the left in the Caribbean have, usually with the benefit of hindsight, been quite critical of the New Jewel Movement. This is particularly true of the left in those countries of the Commonwealth Caribbean in which English-lexicon Creoles are spoken. One of the main criticisms has been that the N.J.M. failed to apply the principles of Marxism-Leninism in a flexible and creative manner. Flexibility and creativity in such a party is only possible in circumstances where there is an active and lively political culture among those thousands of very individual workers, small farmers, etc. who make up the 'masses'. Issues, both local and foreign, have to be understood and freely discussed as a part of ordinary everyday life. This is not possible in circumstances where the bulk of the information about such matters is only available in a language other than the native language of the population, and in which they have only limited competence. Although itself recognising, particularly just prior to October, 1983, that it had a problem of communicating with the population, the N.J.M. did not identify language as an aspect of the problem. Do the critics, operating as they do in societies with very similar language situations, pay any attention to the language question in their own countries?

During the life of the revolution in Grenada, many Creole-speakers would have gone to meetings and mouthed slogans such as 'Down with Imperialism'. It is a sobering thought that many of them were to welcome the U.S. invasion and to rejoice at being 'rescued'. How deep was popular understanding of the policies of the P.R.G. which, on the surface, appeared to have been so widely supported? The political understanding was clearly not as deep as it would have seemed. The existence of the Creole-English diglossia, and the absence of any serious measures to tackle it, must have contributed in some small way to this shallowness of understanding. For every finger pointed by certain critics at Grenada and the N.J.M., three point back. The aim of this work has been to make readers sensitive to the link between the Creole language question and national liberation in the Caribbean. If it has gone any distance in this direction, I will be well satisfied.

References

ABDULAZIZ, M., 1971, 'Tanzania's national language policy and the rise of Swahili political culture', in Whitely, W. (ed.), 1971, *Language Use and Social Change*, Oxford University Press, Oxford.

ALLEYNE, M., 1964, 'Communication between the elite and the masses', in Andic, F., & T. Matthews (eds.), 1965, *The Caribbean in Transition*, Rio Pedras.

ALLEYNE, M., 1980 *Comparative Afro-American*, Karoma Publishers, Ann Arbor.

ALLSOPP, R., 1972, *Why a Dictionary of Caribbean English Usage?*, Caribbean Lexicography Project, University of the West Indies, Cave Hill, Barbados.

ALLSOPP, R., 1978, 'Washing up our wares: Towards a dictionary of our use of English', in Rickford, J. (ed.), 1978, *A Festival of Guyanese Words*, University of Guyana, Georgetown, Guyana.

ALTHUSSER, L., 1971, *Lenin and Philosophy and Other Essays*, New Left Books, London.

THE AMERICAN UNIVERSITY, 1969, *Area Handbook for Guyana*, Johnson Research Associates, Washington, D.C.

ANDERSON, W., and R. DYNES, 1975, *Social Movements, Violence and Changes: The May Movement in Curacao*, Ohio State University Press, Columbus.

ARNOVE, R., 1981, 'The Nicaraguan National Literacy Crusade', in *Comparative Education Review*, Vol. 25, No. 2, pp. 244-260.

BABU, A., 1979, 'Africa and human rights', in *New African*, No. 162, March, 1979, pp. 83-85.

BALIBAR, E., and F. MARCHEREY, 1974, 'Presentation', in Balibar, R., et al., 1974, pp. 9-30

BALIBAR, R. & D. LA PORTE, 1974, *Le Francais National*, Librairie Hachette, Paris.

BARNES, D., 1973, 'Language planning in mainland China: standardisation', in Rubin, J., and R. Shuy (eds.), 1973, *Language Planning: Current Issues and Research*, Georgetown University Press, Washington, D.C.

BÉBEL-GISLER, D., and L. HURBON, 1975 *Culture et Pouvoir dans la Caraïbe*, Librarie-Editions L'Harmattan, Paris.

BEBEL-GISLER, D., 1983, 'De la culture guadeloupéene—De l'indépendance', in *Les Temps Modernes*, Avril-Mai, 1983, pp. 2004-2026.

BENTOLILA, A. and L. GANI, 1981, 'Langues et problèmes d'éducation en Haiti', in *Langages*, Mars, 1981, No. 61, pp. 117-127.

BERRY, P., 1975, 'Literacy and the question of Creole', in Rubin, V., & R. Schaedel (eds.), 1975, *The Haitian Potential*, Teachers' College Press, Columbia University Press, Colombia University Press, New York.

BICKERTON, D., 1975, *Dynamics of a Creole System*, Cambridge University Press, London.

BICKERTON, D., 1981, *Roots of Language*, Karoma Publishers, Ann Arbor.

BISHOP, M., 1984, *In Nobody's Backyard*, Zed Books, London.

BOWEN, G., 1982, '"Local language" creating controversy', in *The Jamaica Daily News*, Nov. 10, 1982.

BRUTUS, E., 1948, *Instruction Publique en Haiti, 1492-1945*, Port-au-Prince.

BUTZER, K., 1978, 'The people of the river', in National Geographic Society, 1978, *Ancient Egypt*, Washington, D.C., pp. 32-41.

CALVET, L.–J., 1973, 'Le colonialisme linguistique en France', in *Les Temps Modernes*, Août-Septembre, 1973, Nos. 324-326. pp. 72-89

CALVET, L.–J., 1974, *Linguistique et Colonialisme*, Payot, Paris.

CARRINGTON, L., 1976, 'Determining language education policy in Caribbean Socio-linguistic complexes', in *International Journal of the Sociology of Language*, 8, pp. 27-44.

CARRINGTON, L., 1978a, 'Language problems in schools of today', in *Trinidad and Tobago Review*, Jan., 1978.

CARRINGTON, L., 1978b, *Education and Development in the English-speaking Caribbean: A Contemporary Survey*, UNESCO/ECLA/UNDP Project on Development and Education in Latin America and the Caribbean, Buenos Aires.

CARRINGTON, L., 1980, *Literacy in the English-speaking Caribbean*, School of Education, University of the West Indies, St. Augustine, Trinidad.

CARRINGTON, L., 1981, *Literacy and Rural Development: A Look at the St. Lucian Initiative*, paper prepared for the ICAE executive meeting and seminar, May—June, 1981, Port-of-Spain, Trinidad.

CARRINGTON, L., 1982, *Rational Language Policy Decisions for the Creole-speaking Caribbean States*, Mimeo, school of Education, University of the West Indies, St. Augustine, Trinidad.

CASSIDY, F., 1978, 'A revised phonemic orthography for Anglophone Caribbean Creoles', in *Proceedings of the Conference of the Society for Caribbean Linguistics,* University of the West Indies, Cave Hill, Barbados, 1978.

CATHOLIC STANDARD, 1982, 'The country is bankrupt, fan-out activists told', March 28, 1982, Georgetown, Guyana, p. 1.

CENSUS RESEARCH PROGRAMME, 1976, *Census of the Commonwealth Caribbean,* University of the West Indies, Jamaica.

COMRIE, B., 1981, *The Languages of the Soviet Union,* Cambridge University Press, Cambridge & London.

CRAIG, D., 1980, 'Language, society and education in the West Indies', in *Caribbean Journal of Education,* Vol. 7, No. 1, Jan., 1980.

CUMMINS, J., 1979, 'Linguistic interdependence and the educational development of bilingual children', In *Review of Educational Research,* Vol. 49, No. 2, 1979, pp. 222-251.

DE FRANCIS, J., 1967, 'Language and script reform', in Sebeok, T. (ed.), 1967, *Current Trends in Linguistics, Vol. 11,* Mouton, the Hague & Paris, pp. 130-150.

DE RONCERAY, H., and S. PETIT-FRERE, 1976, 'Projet expérimental sur le bilinguisme créole-français au niveau de l'enseignement primaire en Haïti', in *Les Cahiers de CHISS,* No. 12, Dec., 1975.

DE VASTEY, P., 1828 (1969), *An Essay on the Causes of the Revolution and Civil Wars of Hayti,* Negro Universities Press, New York.

DEVONISH, H., 1978, *The Selection and Codification of a Widely Understood and Publicly Useable Language Variety in Guyana, to be Used a Vehicle of National Development,* Unpublished D. Phil. dissertation, University of York, England.

DEVONISH, H., 1979, 'The question of what medium of instruction should be used in education: some Third World examples', paper presented to the *National Seminar on Education,* Grenada, July, 1979.

DEVONISH, H., 1980, 'Towards the establishment of an Institute for Creole Language Standardization and Development in the Caribbean', Society for Caribbean Linguistics Conference, Aruba, 1980, in Carrington, L. (ed.), 1983, *Studies in Caribbean Language,* Society for Caribbean Linguistics, University of the West Indies, Trinidad, pp. 300-316.

EDWARDS, W., 1975, *Sociolinguistic Behaviour in Rural and Urban Circumstances in Guyana,* Unpublished D. Phil. dissertation, University of York, England.

EERSEL, C., 1982, 'Sranan in transition', Society for Caribbean Linguistics Conference, Surinam, Sept., 1982.

FANON, F., 1963, *The Wretched of the Earth,* Penguin, Harmondsworth.

152 Hubert Devonish

FARIA, N., 1982, 'Creole alphabet for Dominica', in *Caribbean Contact*, Feb., 1982, p. 2.
FERGUSON, C., 1959, 'Diglossia', in Giglioli, P. (ed.), 1972, *Language in Social Context*, Penguin, Harmondsworth.
FISHMAN, J.A., 1971, *Sociolinguistics: A Brief Introduction*, Rowley, Mass.
FITZGERALD, C., 1961, *China*, Cresset Press, London.
FREIRE, P., 1970, *Cultural Action for Freedom*, Penguin, Harmondsworth.
FREIRE, P., 1971, *Pedagogy of the Oppressed*, Penguin, Harmondsworth.
FREIRE, P., 1973, *Education for Critical Consciousness*, Seabury Press, New York.
FREIRE, P., 1978, *Pedagogy in Process: Letters to Guinea-Bissau*, Seabury Press, New York.
FONTAINE, P., 1982, 'Language, society and development: dialectic of French and Creole use in Haiti', in *Latin American Perspectives*, Vol. VII, No. 1, pp. 28-49.
GANI, L., 1983, 'Réforme éducative et utilité sociale de l'enseignement en Haiti', in *Espace Créole*, No. 5, 1983, pp. 59-74.
GIBSON, K., 1982, *Tense and Aspect in Guyanese Creole*, D. Phil, dissertation, University of York, England.
GORDON, S., 1963, *A Century of West Indian Education*, Longman, London.
GROOTAERS, W., 1967, 'Dialectology', in Sebeok, T.. (ed.), 1967, *Current Trends in Linguistics, Vol. II*, Mouton, The Hague.
GUYANA CHRONICLE, 1982, 'Tell the court what happened then', Sept., 10, 1982.
HALL, N., 1983?, *Empire without Dominion: Denmark and her West Indian Colonies 1671-1848*, Unpublished mimeo, Dept. of History, University of the West Indies, Jamaica.
HANLON, J., 1980, 'A country of illiterates', in *New African*, No. 149, Jan., 1980, pp. 31-32.
HARRIES, L., 1968, 'Swahili in modern East Africa', in Fishman, J. et al. (eds.), 1968, *Language Problems in Developing Nations*, Wiley, New York.
HIRA, S., 1983, 'Class formation and class struggle in Surinam', in Ambursley, F., and R. Cohen (eds.), 1983, *Crisis in the Caribbean*, Heinemann, Kingston, pp. 166-190.
HONORAT, J., 1974, *Enquête sur le Developpement*, Imprimerie Centrale, Port-au-Prince.
HURBON, L., 1983, 'Racisme et sous-produit de racisme', in *Temps Modernes*, Avril–Mai, 1983, No. 441-442, pp. 1988-2003.
JAMES, C.L.R., 1963, *Black Jacobins*, Random House, New York.
JERNUDD, 1981, 'Planning language treatment: linguistics for the

Third World', in *Language and Society,* Vol. 10, No. 1, April, 1981, pp. 43-72.

JEUDA, D., 1983, 'Early Newspaper texts in Papiamentu', in Carrington, L. (ed.), 1983, *Studies in Caribbean Language,* Society for Caribbean Linguistics, University of the West Indies, Trinidad.

JULES, D., 1979, 'Patois folk's cry for justice', in *Caribbean Contact,* March, 1979, p. 9.

KAMERA, W., E. KEZILHABI, and M.R. BESHA, 1976?, *The Socio, Cultural and Economic Factors in Developing a National Language: The Case of Kiswahili in Tanzania,* Mimeo, Dar-es-Salaam.

KEATING, J., 'Radio Central's silly joke', in *The Jamaica Daily News,* Nov., 30, 1982, p. 3.

KEPHART, R., 1979, 'Some background for language planning in Grenada', submitted to the *National Seminar on Education,* Grenada, July, 1979.

KEPHART, R., 1984a, 'Literacy through Creole English: Report on an applied project', presented to the *Conference of the Society for Caribbean Linguistics,* University of the West Indies, Mona, Jamaica, 1984.

KEPHART, R., 1984b, 'An orthography and sample materials for teaching reading in a Creole-speaking community', paper presented to the *Conference on Languages Without a Written Tradition and Their Role in Education.* Thames Polytechnic, August – September, 1984.

KUMBO, S., 1972, 'The role of Swahili in Tanzania as both national and working language', in *Kiswahili,* Vol. 42, No. 1, March, 1972, pp. 39-42.

LATOURETTE, K., 1946, *The Chinese: Their History and Culture,* Macmillan, New York.

LAWAETZ, E., 1980, *Black Education in the Danish West Indies from 1732-1853,* St. Croix Friends of Denmark Society, St. Croix, U.S.V.I.

LEFANU, S., 1981, 'Pulling off the educational miracle', in *New African,* No. 162, March, 1981, p. 181.

LEHMANN, W., 1975, *Language and Linguistics in the People's Republic of China,* University of Texas Press, Austin and London.

LERESTAN, 1981, 'Chimen lanng', an interview with Fr. P. Anthony, in *Grif an Tè,* No. 61, Oct., 23, 1981, pp. 4-5.

LUCKHOO, L., 1977, 'Letter to the editor', *Sunday Chronicle,* Feb., 13, 1977.

MAGLOIRE, S., 1982, *Dominican Creole Usage in the Mass Media etc.,* Unpublished Caribbean Studies dissertation, University of the West Indies, Jamaica.

MANSFIELD, P., 1976, *The Arabs,* Penguin, Harmondsworth.

MARCELLESI, J., 1979, 'Quelques problèmes de l'hégémonie culturelle en France: langues nationales et langues régionales', in *International Journal of the Sociology of Language,* No. 21, 1979, pp. 63-80.

MARCELLESI, J., 1980, 'Bilinguisme, diglossie, hégémonie: problèmes et tâches', *Langages,* No. 61, Mars, 1981, pp. 9-12

McCONNELL, O., and E. SWAN, 1959, *You Can Learn Creole,* Imprimerie du Sauveur, Petit Goâve, Haiti.

MIONI, A., and A. ARNUZZO-LANZWEERT, 1959, 'Sociolinguistics in Italy', in *International Journal of the Sociology of Language,* No. 21, pp. 81-107.

MORDECAI, P., 1979, *Some Comments on Educational Policy in Creole Speaking and Other Oral Mode Communities with Particular Reference to the Caribbean,* Mimeo.

N.J.M. (New Jewel Movement), 1983, *Minutes of Central Committee Meeting of 14-16 September, 1983,* Mimeo.

NICHOLLS, D., 1979, *From Dessalines to Duvalier,* Cambridge University Press, Cambridge.

NOOR, A., 1979, 'Education lending for the poor', in *Finance and Development,* Vol. 16, No. 2, June, 1979.

O'BARR, J., 1976, 'The evolution of Tanzanian political institutions', in W. & J. O'Barr (eds.), 1976, *Language and Politics,* Mouton, The Hague & Paris, pp. 69-84.

O'SHAUGHNESSY, H., 1984, *Grenada: Revolution, Invasion and Aftermath,* Sphere Books, London.

PERSON, Y., 1973, 'Imperialisme linguistique et colonialisme', in *Les Temps Modernes,* Nos. 324-326, Août-Septembre, 1973, pp. 90-118.

PIERRE-CHARLES, G., 1972, 'Interpretation des faits et perspective du developpement économique en Haïti, in *Culture et Developpement en Haiti,* 1972, Symposium Haiti, Ottawa.

PROSPECTUS OF THE UNIVERSITY OF DAR-ES-SALAAM, 1975-76, Dar-es-Salaam.

PRUDENT, L., 1983a, 'La langue créole aux Antilles et en Guyane', in *Temps Modernes,* Nos. 441-442, Avril–Mai, 1983, pp. 2072-2089.

PRUDENT, L., 1983b, 'Le discours créoliste contemporain: apories et entéléchies', in *Espace Créole,* No. 5, 1983, pp. 31-42.

REINECKE, J., 1975, *A Bibliography of Pidgin and Creole Languages,* University Press of Hawaii, Honolulu.

RICKFORD, J., 1979, *Variation in a Creole Continuum: Quantitative and Implicational Approaches,* Unpublished Ph.D. dissertation, University of Pennsylvania.

RICKFORD, 1983, *Standard and Non-standard Language Attitudes in a Creole Continuum,* Occasional Paper 16, Society for Caribbean Linguistics.

RODNEY, W., 1979, *People's Power, No Dictator,* Working People's Alliance, Georgetown, Guyana.

SCHIROKAUER, C., 1978, *A Brief History of Chinese and Japanese Civilizations,* Harcourt Brace Jovanovich Inc., New York.

SEARLE, C., 1984, *Words Unchained: Language and Revolution in Grenada,* Zed Books, London.

Seminar on an Orthography for St. Lucian Creole, March 1981, Folk Research Centre and Caribbean Research Centre, Castries, St. Lucia.

SHIRŎ, H., 1967, 'Descriptive linguistics in Japan', in Sebeok, T. (ed.), 1067, *Current Trends in Linguistics, Vol. II,* Mouton, The Hague, pp. 530-584.

SHIVJI, I., 1976, *Class Struggles in Tanzania,* Monthly Review Press, New York.

SMALLING, D., 1983, *An Investigation into the Intelligibility of Radio News Broadcasts in Jamaica,* Unpublished Caribbean Studies dissertation, University of the West Indies, Mona, Jamaica.

SOLCHANYK, R., 1982, 'Russian language and Soviet politics', in *Soviet Studies,* Vol. XXXIV, No. 1, January, 1982, pp. 23-42.

SOLOMON, D., 1972, 'Form, content and the post-creole continuum', paper presented to the *Conference on Creole Languages and Educational Development,* 1972, University of the West Indies, Trinidad.

SOTIROPOULOS, D., 1982, 'The social roots of the Greek diglossia', in *Language Problems and Language Planning,* Vol. 6, No. 1, 1982, pp. 1-28.

STONE, C., 1980, *Democracy and Clientelism in Jamaica,* Transaction Books, New Brunswick and London.

SUNDAY CHRONICLE, 1981, 'Everyday usage of English in Guyana', 26th April, 1981.

THOMAS, J.J., 1969 (1869), *Theory and Practice of a Creole Grammar,* New Beacon Book Ltd., London and Port-of-Spain.

TODD-DANDARE, R., 1979, 'Analysing variations in Creole languages: the Papiamento-case', paper presented to the *Conference on Theoretical Orientations in Creole Languages,* St. Thomas, 1979.

TODD-DANDARE R., 1980a, Expériences resultant de l'introduction du Papiamento dans le système d'éducation d'Iles Sous le Vent des Antilles Néerlandaises', in Valdman, A. (ed.), *Créole et Enseignement Primaire en Haïti,* Indiana University, Indiana, pp. 9-17

TODD-DANDARE R., 1980b, 'A short survey of the social history of Papiamento', paper presented to the *Conference of the Society for Caribbean Linguistics,* Aruba, 1980.

TODD-DANDARE R., 1982, 'La situacion linguistica en las antillas holandesas', paper presented to the *Conference on Cultural Integration in the Caribbean Region,* Kingston, Jamaica, March, 1982.

TROUILLOT, H., 1979?, *Les Limites du Créole dans notre Enseignement,* Imprimerie des Antilles, Port-au-Prince.

TRUDGILL, P., 1979, 'Standard and non-standard dialects of
English in the United Kingdom: problems and policies', in
International Journal of the Sociology of Language, No. 21,
1979, pp. 9-24.

U.P.L.G. (Union Populaire pour la Libération de la Guadeloupe),
1982, 'La situation politique en Guadeloupe depuis le 10 Mai',
in Les Temps Modernes, Nos. 441-442, Avril-Mai, 1983, pp.
1961-1973.

U.T.A. (Union des Travailleurs Agricoles), 1983, 'Entretien avec
un responsable de l'U.T.A.', in *Les Temps Modernes,* Avril–
Mai, 1983, No. 441-442, pp. 1974-1986.

VALDMAN, A., 1978, *Langue créole: statut, structure et origines,*
Klincksieck, Paris.

VALDMAN, A., 1982, 'Educational reform and the instrumentali-
sation of the vernacular in Haiti', in Hartford, B., et al. (eds.), 1982,
International Bilingual Education: The Role of the Vernacular,
Plenum Press, New York.

VANROMPAY, M., 1980, 'Experience in Creole education', *Society for Caribbean Linguistics Conference,* Aruba, September,
1980.

VERNET, P., 1980, *Techniques d'Ecriture du Créole Haïtien,*
Imprimerie Le Natal, S.A.

VIKOR, L., 1974, 'Language standardisation and nationalism', in
*Papers from the Conference on the Standardisation of Asian
Languages,* Manila, Philippines, December 16-24, 1974,
Australian National University.

VOORHOEVE, J., 1971, 'Varieties of Creole in Surinam', in
Hymes, D. (ed.), 1971, *Pidginisation and Creolisation of
Languages,* Cambridge University Press, London, pp. 303-
315..

VOORHOEVE, J. and U. LICHVELD (eds.), 1975 *Creole Drum:
An Anthology of Creole Literature in Surinam,* Yale University
Press, New Haven and London.

WHITELEY, W., 1968, 'Ideal and reality in national language
policy: a case for Tanzania', in Fishman, J.A. et al. (eds.), 1968,
Language Problems of Developing Nations, Wiley, New York.

WILSON, D., 1977, 'Rationale of a West Indian language arts
course for primary schools', in *Caribbean Journal of Education,* Vol. 4, No. 3, September, 1977.

W.P.A. (Working People's Alliance), 1979, *Toward a Revolutionary
Socialist Guyana,* W.P.A. Georgetown Guyana.

WOMEN'S DESK, 1979, 'Memo 24: recommendations on educational reform in Grenada', paper presented to the *National
Seminar on Education,* Grenada, July, 1979.

YANSEN, C., 1975, *Random Remarks on Creolese,* published by
   author.
ZANDRONIS, D., 1981, 'Pour ou contre le Créole a l'école', *Le
   Magazine Guadeloupéen,* No. 2, Dec., 1981—Jan., 1982, pp.
   26-36.

Some Books Published by Karia Press

Available through Bookshops or direct from Karia Press, BCM Karia, London, WC1N 3XX, United Kingdom. Tel: (01) - 249 4446

For direct orders, enclose payment with order. (Also add handling charge of 15% UK; 20% Overseas)

Short Stories/ Prose Fiction

Song For Simone
and other stories

by Jacob Ross

ISBN 0 946918 29 5 Pb £3.95
ISBN 0 946918 33 3 Hb £8.95

The Day Sharon Lost Her Way Home

by Jennifer Martin
Illustrated by Paul Dash

ISBN 0 946918 23 6 Pb £3.95
ISBN 0 946918 24 4 Hb £5.95

The Earliest Patriots:
Being the true adventures of certain survivors of Bussa's Rebellion' (1816), in the island of Barbados and Abroad

by Evelyn O'Callaghan

ISBN 0 946918 53 8 Pb £2.95

Afrikan Lullaby
Folk Tales From Zimbabwe

by Chisiya

ISBN 0 946918 45 7 Pb £1.95

Biography/ Autobiography

The Autobiography of A Zimbabwean Woman

by Sekai Nzenza

ISBN 0 946918 21 X Pb £4.95
ISBN 0 946918 22 8 Hb £8.95

Dispossessed Daughter of Africa

by Carol Trill

ISBN 0 946918 42 2 Pb £4.95
ISBN 0 946918 42 0 Hb £8.95

In Troubled Waters
Memoirs of my Seventy Years in England

by Ernest Marke

ISBN 0 946918 2 5 Pb £4.95

"I Think of My Mother"
Notes on the Life and Times of Claudia Jones

by Buzz Johnson

ISBN 0 946918 02 3 Pb £3.95
ISBN 0 946918 05 8 Hb £8.95

This list represents some books already in print and those soon to be published. For a full list of published and forthcoming publications please write to the address above.

Black People in Britain

We Are Our Own Educators!
Josina Machel: From Supplementary to Black Complementary School

by Valentino A. Jones

ISBN 0 946918 37 6 Pb £3.95

Telling The Truth
The Life and Times of the British Honduran Forestry Unit in Scotland (1941-44)

by Amos Ford

ISBN 0 946918 01 5 Pb £2.95
ISBN 0 946918 03 1 Hb £7.95

Many Struggles
West-Indian Workers and Service Personnel in Britain 1939-45

by Marika Sherwood

ISBN 0 946918 04 X Pb £3.95
ISBN 0 946918 00 7 Hb £8.95

Language

Caribbean & African Languages:
Social History Language, Literature and Education

by Morgan Dalphinis

ISBN 0 946918 06 6 Pb £6.95
ISBN 0 946918 07 4 Hb £16.95

Language and Liberation:
Creole Language Politics in the Caribbean

by Hubert Devonish

ISBN 0 946918 27 9 Pb £5.95
ISBN 0 946918 27 8 Hb £9.95

New Poetry

Because The Dawn Breaks!
Poems Dedicated to the Grenadian People

by Merle Collins
With Introduction by
Ngũgĩ Wa Thiong'o

ISBN 0 946918 08 2 Pb £3.95
ISBN 0 946918 09 0 Hb £8.95

For Those Who Will Come After!

by Morgan Dalphinis

ISBN 0 946918 10 4 Pb £3.95
ISBN 0 946918 11 2 Hb £8.95

Word Rhythms From the Life of A Woman

by Elean Thomas

ISBN 0 946918 40 6 Pb £3.95
ISBN 0 946918 41 4 Hb £8.95

Rapso Explosion

by Bro. Resistance

ISBN 0 946918 34 1 Pb £3.95